UNSCRIPTED LEARNING

UNSCRIPTED LEARNING

Using Improv Activities Across the K-8 Curriculum

CARRIE LOBMAN
MATTHEW LUNDQUIST

Teachers College, Columbia University
New York and London

Published by Teachers College Press, 1234 Amsterdam Avenue, New York, NY 10027

Library of Congress Cataloging in Publication Information:

Lobman, Carrie.
Unscripted learning : using improv activities across the K–8 curriculum /
    Carrie Lobman and Matthew Lundquist.
p. cm.
Includes bibliographical references and index.
ISBN 978-0-8077-4797-1 (pbk. : alk. paper)
ISBN 978-0-8077-4798-8 (cloth : alk. paper)
1. Effective teaching. 2. Improvisation (Acting) I. Lundquist, Matthew. II. Title.
LB1025.3.L62 2007
371.39'9–dc22   2006103036

978-0-8077-4797-1 (pbk : alk. paper)
978-0-8077-4798-8 (cloth : alk. paper)

Printed on acid-free paper.
Manufactured in the United States of America.

14   13   12   11   10   09   08   07   8   7   6   5   4   3   2   1

This book is dedicated to
Dr. Lois Holzman
Methodologist, Mentor, Friend

Contents

Foreword

Creativity is the watchword of the 21st century. Widely read writers like *New York Times* columnist Thomas L. Friedman (*The World is Flat*) and best-selling author Daniel H. Pink (*A Whole New Mind*) have described a transformed global economy in which creative people and societies will come out on top. Richard Florida (*The Rise of the Creative Class*) has documented the nature of creative work in today's economy, and has identified the key characteristics of those countries and regions that are most likely to generate innovation.

In recent years, Washington pundits and corporate CEOs have joined the conversation with two influential reports. In 2005, the Council on Competitiveness released a report titled *Innovate America* and another influential group, the Business Roundtable, released the report *Tapping America's Potential: The Education for Innovation Initiative*. These reports firmly placed the issue of innovation on the desk of every top CEO and university chancellor in this United States. In response, a bipartisan group of U.S. senators introduced a bill titled "The National Innovation Act of 2005" (S. 2109; the bill did not become law).

What's missing from all of these high-visibility reports and discussions is the voice of the educators who, everyone agrees, are a critical link in making it all happen. Only teachers can build classrooms and activities that foster creativity in students. Only school leaders can transform their institutions to reward creative teaching and support radical new methods. Only school boards and state departments of education can rewrite the high-stakes tests required by No Child Left Behind so that creativity is not left behind. If our tests measure only the memorization of facts and rote procedures, then schools and teachers ultimately have very little room for creativity in the classroom.

I think the most promising way to build creative schools is to borrow from the performing arts. After all, teaching has long been compared to performance: teachers stand "on stage" in front of the classroom "audience"; the lesson plan and textbook are "scripts" for the performance; teachers "rehearse" their presentations; and the teacher-performer must use timing, stage presence, and enthusiasm to hold the attention of the student-audience. This metaphor emphasizes important skills for teachers, such as presentation, delivery, voice, movement, and timing. Yet the metaphor of teaching-as-performance has a critical problem: It suggests a solo performer reading from a script with the students as a passive, observing audience.

In the book you are holding in your hands, Carrie Lobman and Matthew Lundquist offer a solution to this problem: Consider teaching to be *improvisational* performance. An improvising teacher interacts with and responds to the class. The flow of the class is unpredictable and emerges from the actions of all participants, teachers and students alike. Students participate creatively in the performance, rather than sitting passively and observing the teacher's solo performance. This book provides very specific and concrete advice to help teachers create an improvisational classroom.

The most important thing to know about improvisation is that it's an ensemble art. Several actors go up on stage without a script and without having discussed what they're going to do. Then they entertain an audience for 1 or 2 hours, creating characters, relationships, plot lines, and believable dialogue. No single actor is ever in control; instead, actors are taught to trust in the wisdom of the group and to allow relationship dynamics and plot twists to emerge, unexpectedly and unpredictably, from the flow of the dialogue.

"Collective intelligence" and "the wisdom of crowds" are the buzzwords of today's Internet economy. The hottest companies are social networking sites that help thousands of people build links among their friends and colleagues (MySpace, FaceBook, LinkedIn). Sites like del.icio.us and Google harness collective intelligence to help each of us find exactly the information we need. Innovation in today's economy is always a collaborative act, and that's why teachers have to foster collaborative creativity to engender creativity in their students. Improv is more than just an obscure genre of theater; it represents the purest form of collective intelligence.

In *Unscripted Learning*, Lobman and Lundquist have pulled off a difficult task: They've written an easy-to-read, practical handbook for teachers. As they say, it's an "improv manual." Over the last decades, many reference books have been published that describe improv exercises and games for actors, but those books aren't very helpful for teachers because the exercises they contain generally assume prior experience in theater and are not specifically designed to enhance learning. This book is a reference that teachers will want to keep right on their desk in the classroom. It starts with very general improv exercises that build trust and group spirit, and then moves on to chapters that are specific to various content areas: literacy, math, social studies, and science. Unlike professional actors, these exercises are designed for use in classrooms, not on stage with an audience. For each exercise, the authors start by specifying the appropriate grade level, the amount of time it will take, and the materials required. It's obvious that Lobman and Lundquist have a lot of experience using these same activities in their own classrooms: They are careful to address issues that teachers face every day, such as assessment, classroom safety, and children with special needs.

At the same time, this book is grounded in solid, up-to-the-minute research and theory. Improv isn't just a flighty activity for artsy types; it has the potential to teach students the core collaborative skills that are absolutely necessary for success in today's innovation economy. In my own scientific publications, I've argued that improvisation can help us to understand and to improve teaching (Sawyer, 2004, 2006), and Lobman and Lundquist follow the same general approach using accessible language that can be understood by any teacher.

Kudos to Carrie Lobman and Matthew Lundquist for writing a book that's needed, that's academically solid, and, most of all, that will be helpful to teachers.

— R. Keith Sawyer, Washington University in St. Louis

REFERENCES

Business Roundtable. (2005). *Tapping America's potential: The education for innovation initiative*. Washington, DC: Business Roundtable.

Council on Competitiveness. (2005). *Innovate America: National innovation initiative summit and report*. Washington, DC: Council on Competitiveness.

Florida, R. (2002). *The rise of the creative class and how it's transforming work, leisure, community, and everyday life*. New York: Basic Books.

Friedman, T. L. (2005). *The world is flat: A brief history of the twenty-first century*. New York: Farrar, Straus, and Giroux.

Pink, D. H. (2005). *A whole new mind: Why right-brainers will rule the future*. New York: Riverhead Books.

Sawyer, R. K. (2004). Creative teaching: Collaborative discussion as disciplined improvisation. *Educational Researcher, 33*(2), 12–20.

Sawyer, R. K. (2006). Educating for innovation. *The International Journal of Thinking Skills and Creativity, 1*(1), 41–48.

Preface

Improv theater in the United States has a long-standing relationship with children and education. In the 1920s and 1930s, Viola Spolin, who is sometimes credited with "inventing" improv in the United States, developed a series of theater games to use with young people to help them be more successful learners. Spolin's games went on to become the foundation of modern adult improv comedy. Despite its beginnings as a series of exercises for children, improv is rarely used in educational settings and very few teachers are aware of the relationship between improvisation and learning. Improv remains the province of specialized theater teachers or classroom teachers who happen to have an acting background. This is a loss for children and teachers alike. Improv is too valuable a learning tool to only be used by specialists. The goal of this book is to put this useful tool into the hands of many more teachers, teacher educators, and, by extension, the children with whom they work.

We have written this book because, as teachers and teacher educators, we have found improvisation to be a wonderfully effective learning tool for elementary and middle school classrooms. This book is divided into two parts. Part One, which includes Chapters 1 and 2, is a theoretical introduction to improv and contains guidelines for doing improv with children. Part Two consists of detailed descriptions of over 100 improv activities, categorized by content area, and includes recommendations for using them in the classroom.

Chapter 1 introduces improvisation as a learning methodology and as a way of bringing creative, collective activity into the classroom. It provides readers with a rationale for doing improv in the classroom based on a Vygotskian-influenced understanding of learning as the doing of what we do not yet know how to do and as the creation of zones of proximal development. Learning, as discussed in this chapter and then further articulated in the rest of the book, should not be confined to the activity of acquiring knowledge and skills but should also include working collaboratively, taking risks, and doing what you don't yet know how to do. This chapter illustrates how improv activities can help create a collaborative, supportive learning environment even within the constraints of traditional school cultures.

Whereas Chapter 1 is about the theoretical importance of improvisation for learning, Chapter 2 presents the nuts and bolts of how to do improv in the classroom. It is aimed specifically at those teachers (and teachers-in-training) who have no improv or theater experience. Chapter 2 introduces readers to the fundamental principles of improv theater. In the chapter, we describe each of these principles and give several examples of their use in various contexts. The chapter also provides guidelines for how to introduce improv in the classroom and offers advice on how to set up the physical environment, explain and demonstrate the activities, direct the activities, and help children with special needs or who are shy or appear reticent participate.

The second half of this book contains six chapters, each of which includes improv activities that are useful in addressing different elements of classroom life or particular subject areas. Each of these chapters has

- an introduction that links the topic of the chapter and improvisation
- a framework for understanding the skills that are developed when children learn these particular improv activities
- guidelines for choosing between the different activities
- detailed descriptions of the activities, including a legend showing the appropriate age range, improv skill level, time required, and necessary materials for each activity; a few sentences providing an overview of each activity and the skills that can be learned by participating in it; step-by-step directions for introducing each activity to children; hints for how to lead each activity; examples of "side coaching" that can be done to help students be successful; and extension activities for developing additional skills.

Chapter 3, "Creating the Ensemble," focuses on building an improvisational learning environment in the classroom. It includes activities that are specifically aimed at learning to work as a group or an ensemble and exploring the language of emotionality and its various expressions.

Chapters 4 through 6 provide activities that are designed to complement existing curricula and develop skills in basic areas of learning in the elementary and middle grades. Chapter 4, "Improvising Language and Literacy," presents activities that help build literacy skills such as phonemic awareness, storytelling, playing with words and sounds, listening, and comprehension. Chapter 5, "Improvising Math," gives children an opportunity to play with numbers, shapes, and measurements. Chapter 6, "Improv in the Content Areas," presents activities that are appropriate for science and social studies curricula. The book concludes with a final chapter, "More Advanced Scene Work," that provides opportunities for classes that choose to take their improvisational skills further by learning some more advanced performance-style games.

While the book is organized around subjects, please don't feel constrained by that structure. Our primary goal is to help teachers bring creativity and playfulness into their teaching. So, play with the book; use it in any way that you find useful. Skip around and pull games from different chapters. Play a few games and then read the introduction. Use the activities in this book as a jumping-off point and create your own improv games with your students. In the language of improv, this book is an *offer*.

Acknowledgments

This book is but a moment in an improvised, collective process. It is the product of years of work by hundreds of people around the world who are bringing into existence a new psychology and, by extension, a performatory learning model that aims to bring development into school environments that are sorely lacking in creativity.

We owe a particular debt to four brilliant people whose work has shaped and guided our practice: Lev Vygotsky, the early 20th-century Russian psychologist; Fred Newman and Lois Holzman, who have brought Vygotsky's work into the 21st century; and Christine LaCerva, a pioneer in improvisational therapeutic and educational practices with children and adolescents.

We are grateful to the following people and institutions for their help and support:

- The East Side Institute, Performance of a Lifetime, Rutgers University, and Bank Street College of Education
- Sean Adcroft, Jeff Bergman, Jane Bolgatz, Lola Broomberg, Lisa Dombrow, Liz Eckert, Mary Fridley, Nancy Green, Christine Helm, Maureen Kelly, Kat Koppett, Gwen Lowenheim, Maralyn Lowenheim, Joan Mahon-Powell, Susan Massad, Melissa Meyer, Paul Murray, David Nackman, Tony Perone, Sharon Ryan, Cathy Salit, Amy Samelson, Keith Sawyer, Melea Seward, Andrea Spencer, Phil Terry, Ellen Wictor, and Jan Wootten

We have been fortunate for the guidance of two experienced and skilled editors at Teachers College Press, Sue Liddicoat and Marie Ellen Larcada, both of whom have provided guidance throughout this process. We'd also like to thank the talented production team for bringing the physical book into existence.

Finally, to the children and educators who continue to amaze and inspire us with their willingness to play.

UNSCRIPTED LEARNING

Chapter 1

Improvisation and Learning: Why Do Improv in the Classroom?

Doing improv comedy exercises and scene work in the classroom is a wonderful tool for creating a positive learning environment. In order to learn, human beings have to do what we don't yet know how to do—in other words, we have to take risks. Improv is about learning to take risks and, even more important, it's about learning how to support other people to take risks. We've written this book to tell you why this activity is so effective in the classroom and to show you how to do it with the students in your class.

Improv is also about learning how to work as an ensemble—as a group. That is what classes are—they are groups of people coming together every day for the purpose of learning, whether it be learning to read or learning about the water cycle. How can teachers help their classes work together effectively as a group? What skills do students need to develop to be able to do this? It turns out that they need to be able to do many of the things that theatrical improvisers do. They need to be able to listen to one another—not impatiently or politely waiting for their turn to talk, but listening in order to use what other people say to move the work of the group forward. They need to be able to work cooperatively, not competitively. When a class improvises together they learn how to work together, to create together, to create learning and learners.

Improv has gained a lot of popularity in the last few years. There are improv groups performing on TV and in comedy clubs. And improv is no longer the sole property of the entertainment industry. All over the country, thousands of people are discovering that learning to improvise can be transformative to their personal and professional lives. Improv classes are now available in most cities and have also become an important training tool in the business world, as corporations try to help their employees adapt to a rapidly changing world. People have discovered that learning to improvise can help people become strong leaders who are able to make use of the creative potential of groups of people. At any bookstore one can find several how-to books on improv.

So why did we decide to write this particular book? Both of us are classroom teachers and staff developers, and we have used the improv activities in this book in our classrooms with children and in our work with teachers. Our goal in writing this book is to provide teachers (even

1

those with no improv or theater experience) with an improv manual that is especially designed for them—that provides activities that are age-appropriate, fun, and described in such a way that they can be easily understood and explained to children. While this book is primarily a practical guide to doing improv in the classroom, it is also a rationale for why improv is a valuable activity. This first chapter is an introduction to improv and its relationship to learning and development. It provides a theoretical framework for why improv is useful in the classroom. As everyone knows, it is important for teachers to understand and be able to articulate to others why they do what they do. We hope this chapter will be helpful in this regard.

HUMAN BEINGS ARE IMPROVISERS

While people sometimes think of improvisation as being synonymous with impulsiveness—as saying or doing the first thing that comes to mind—improvisation as a cultural art form is not about "anything goes." In music, theater, and dance, improvisation is choosing to create something (usually with other people) by making use of whatever is available.

People tend to think that this kind of improvisation belongs onstage and is the sole domain of skilled actors and musicians, but human beings actually improvise all the time. No one is given a script at birth and advised to memorize their lines before they participate in life. Everyone improvises every day—when we smile at others on the street, when we choose what to eat for breakfast, and when we engage in conversations. While people often live their lives as if there is a script, the fact is that people are also capable of breaking from the expected. Right at this moment, you could choose to do something unexpected—you could flip this book upside down and begin reading it from the back, or you could turn to the stranger sitting next to you on the bus and say something in a made-up language. Tomorrow in class you and your students could spend the day learning the latest video games. While there are obviously cultural, societal, and legal limitations on what people can and will do, this does not negate the human ability to be improvisational. In addition, no one is a solo performer standing alone in the spotlight. Everyone is part of many improvisational ensembles—with the people on the bus, with families and friends, and with the people with whom we teach and learn.

Paradoxically, despite the fact that there is no script, people often see themselves as being in set roles and as playing a part in an already written play—they are the loving mother, the angry boss, the bored student, the bad reader, or the strict teacher. Rather than creatively improvising our lives all the time, people often stick to what they already know. This lack of creativity not only makes it frustrating when things don't go according to plan, but more than that, set roles and scripts can seriously limit learning and development. This is because for children (and adults), learning and growing involves breaking from what one ordinarily does and doing something new.

While all human beings are improvisers and all of human life includes improvisation, people can get better at improvising when it is done deliberately and consciously. If we teach children the skills and techniques used by professional improvisers, they can become more creative learners.

WHAT IS IMPROV?

Improvisation, as distinct from other practices in the theater arts, is unscripted performance. Improvisers may prepare themselves physically and mentally, but they do not know what will happen in a scene before it is performed. In improv comedy, the basis for the activities in this book, the performers work collectively to create an unscripted scene or story. Since 1998 many people have become familiar with improv comedy through the television show *Whose Line Is It Anyway?* On this program, and in improv shows and classes across the world, a group of performers uses suggestions from the audience as the jumping-off point for creating intricate and often hilarious skits on the spot.

Much of what makes improvisation unexpected and interesting is the way the ensemble works together. A careful observer of improvisational groups will recognize that the most skilled members of the ensemble are often not the ones who receive the most laughs or appear to contribute the most. The real talent in improvisation is expressed by supporting the ensemble. This is accomplished most effectively through the recognition, acceptance, and giving of offers. An offer is something a performer does—a movement, facial expression, gesture, utterance, and so forth—with which the members of the ensemble create a scene.

A well-tuned ensemble will say yes to one another's offers. This can be done literally or figuratively, through completely accepting any offer that is brought onstage and adding something new to it. Often improvisers have the experience of embracing offers that take them in directions that are far from what they might have had in mind. For example, if two improvisers are onstage and the first one says, "I've been getting these horrible headaches," he is probably assuming that he is talking to his doctor or a friend. However, if his partner responds, "I don't care if you are bleeding internally, if you don't get back to work you are fired," it becomes clear that he is talking to his boss, and he works to go with that offer. The best improvisers learn to love these moments. A large part of what makes improv so interesting is watching the ensemble create something by working together rather than competing with one another.

While we think of improv as the province of professional performers and theater classes, it turns out that learning to improvise can be valuable for all sorts of groups, and in particular for groups of students and teachers. Every day in classrooms around the country teachers help their students work together effectively so that everyone can learn. In addition to math, reading, and social studies, teachers want children to learn how to learn—how to take risks, be creative, try new things, and listen to one another and to adults. Improv gives teachers and students a set of tools for creating this kind of supportive and creative learning environment where everyone can contribute what they can in order to help everyone learn.

DOING WHAT YOU DON'T KNOW HOW TO DO

Learning is often thought of acquisitionally, or in terms of *what* is learned. We acquire skills and knowledge. We learn about things and we learn how to do things. We learn how to do multiplication, we learn about American history. Of course it's important that children acquire knowledge and skills, but learning is not just acquisition, and helping children learn is not just about the what but also about the *how*. It's about the activity of learning.

As classroom teachers and authors of this book, our understanding of the how has been most influenced by the work of the psychologist Lev Vygotsky and the philosopher Ludwig Wittgenstein, and further developed by the social therapists Fred Newman and Lois Holzman. They have built on Vygotsky's and Wittgenstein's theories to create a new understanding and practice of human learning and development used to create successful therapeutic and educational programs including an independent elementary school, supplemental education programs, a group therapy practice, and a school-based mental health clinic. In these programs young (and not so young) people create environments where they can do what they do not know how to do. Among these many programs is the East Side Institute for Group and Short Term Psychotherapy, a research and training center in New York City where we have studied and been trained in an improvisational approach to teaching and learning.

The activity of learning involves doing what you do not know how to do, which is not the same as pretending you know what you are doing. Pretending you know what you are doing is often detrimental to learning. It keeps you from asking questions or getting help because you are trying not to be found out. Doing what you don't know how to do, on the other hand, is about taking risks and doing new things, not just sticking with what you already know.

If you only do what you know how to do you can get better at what you already know, but it is not possible to do something qualitatively different. For example, if you know how to play the piano, you can keep getting better and better at it, but this does not mean that you will be able to play the violin. In order to start playing the violin you would have to do what you did not know how to do (which is, after all, how you learned to play the piano in the first place!). The skills you had as a piano player would probably be helpful to you, but you could not just rely on them. You could read books on playing the violin and watch violin players, but sooner or later you would have to pick up the violin and play without knowing exactly what to do.

This is how we all learn when we are infants and very young children. Prior to coming to school, children are always doing what they do not know how to do, in part because they do not know how to do very much. For example, when a baby is first learning how to speak, her parents do not hand her a grammar book and tell her to get back to them when she is talking in full sentences. The baby says, "Ga, ba, dooo, ga" and her father says, "You miss Mommy, let's look out the window and see if she is coming home yet." One way of understanding what people do when they talk with a baby is that they relate to her as who she is and who she is becoming at the same time. They do not insist that the baby speak like an adult (who she will be), and they do not relate to the baby as a nonspeaker (who she is); they include the baby as a participant in their conversations and in that process she becomes a speaker.

Even after children leave infancy and grow into toddlers and preschoolers, they continue to be supported to do what they do not know how to do. When a 3-year-old picks up a book and "reads" to her parents, they do not question her ability to read or tell her that she is not *really* reading. They sit with rapt attention and take a picture to send to Grandma. It is by being related to as who they are *and* who they are becoming that children learn the myriad of things that they learn how to do before they ever arrive at school.

Of all the things that very young children learn, one of the most important is that they learn that they are learners. What does this mean? When people talk to babies as becoming-speakers and preschoolers as becoming-readers, the babies and preschoolers experience that learning involves creatively imitating those around you and that it requires doing things without knowing how to do them. In these environments, where they are not judged on what they already know and where whatever they do or say is related to as valuable and useful (in improv terms, as an offer), children learn that they are learners. They learn that they are capable of changing, growing, and doing new things.

In general, this is not the kind of learning that dominates once children are in school. School learning is often structured around the accumulation and fine-tuning of knowledge rather than the teaching of children that they are learners. What becomes important is to have the students demonstrate in various ways what they have learned, and often the pressure to do so deprives children of the experiences of being and becoming learners. Over time some children come to be seen by themselves and others as good learners and others as bad learners, and still others become skilled at looking like they know what they are doing when they are not really learning anything. Children develop an identity. Once acquired, these identities are hard to get rid of. There are not a lot of opportunities to continuously learn that you are a learner. This book is about creating those kinds of learning environments in the classroom.

VYGOTSKY AND THE ZONE OF PROXIMAL DEVELOPMENT

In the first half of the 20th century the Russian psychologist Lev Vygotsky gave a name to social environments where people can go beyond their current level of development. He called them Zones of Proximal Development (ZPD). Vygotsky argued that if people only focus on what the child can do independently, then they will only see what has already developed and they will miss what is developing. He pointed out that children are able to do many more things within a supportive social context than they can do alone. Over the years there have been many interpretations of the ZPD. Some psychologists and educators have focused on the instrumental value of the ZPD as a teaching technique for helping an individual child do what is a little beyond her or his independent skill level by being supported by an adult or a more skilled peer.

Others, we among them, see the ZPD as a creative, improvisational activity. The ZPD is the activity of people creating environments where children (and adults) can take risks, make mistakes, and support one another to do what they do not yet know how to do. From this perspective the ZPD is not a technique, or even a distance. It is an activity, an activity that people engage in together. It is by participating in creating environments where learning can occur that children learn.

In order to illustrate what we mean by the ZPD being the activity of creating the environment for learning and the learning itself, let's look at what young children are doing when they are engaged in pretend play, say Spider-Man. No one hands them the rules for Spider-Man, assigns parts, and tells everyone what to say. The group of children creates the environment for the game and plays the game at the same time. If they do not create the conditions to be able to play Spider-Man—if, for example, they never find a way to decide who will be Spider-Man or if they all go off and do their own thing—there will be no game. Many educators and psychologists have pointed out that it is this feature of play—the fact that the players themselves create it—that makes play such a great way for children to learn and develop. Vygotsky identified this kind of social play as a ZPD for preschool-age children.

LEARNING AND IMPROVISATION

What are children doing when they pretend with each other? What are the baby and her family doing when they are babbling together? They are improvising. They are not following a script. They are using what is available to them, namely themselves and their varying experiences, as the material to create an improvised performance together. That is how people do what they don't know how to do: They improvise.

However, for the most part, the learning and teaching that goes on in school is not improvisational. Rather than creating the environment where risks can be taken, where children can be who they are not, where children can co-create the environment for learning, schools tend to be environments where doing what one *knows* how to do is valued. Those who are good at math raise their hand to answer the questions. Those who are not, don't. If someone is good at making the class laugh and getting yelled at by the teacher, then he or she does that. Everyone is doing what they know how to do, and there is not a lot of improvising going on.

In the classroom children are not always related to, nor do they relate to themselves, as participants in creating the learning environment. They do not often take responsibility for their learning in the way that a few years earlier they took responsibility for creating their play. You could be thinking, "Well, of course this is the case. Children want to play, but they don't necessarily want to learn math." However, it is a rare child who comes to school not wanting to learn. What changes is not so much the desire on the part of the children, but the message that this is not play—this is not like pretending to be Spider-Man. This is someone else's game, and it's called work.

Doing improv in the classroom brings some of the environment of the baby learning to speak or the preschoolers playing Spider-Man into school without the total chaos that might ensue if we all played Spider-Man all day long. We often think of improv as organized pretend play. It provides the learning benefits of the pretend play of preschoolers, but with the organization and challenge that older children are now capable of handling and that the school environment demands.

WE ARE ALL PERFORMERS

Another way to understand the relationship between improv and play is that they are two examples of our human ability to perform. Actually, in our culture, for the most part, performance has come to be seen as the exclusive territory of very young children and skilled actors. Actors are considered professionals whose job it is to create characters that go beyond the identity of the actor, and young children are supported to be who they are not so that they can come to learn who they are. However, it is possible and useful to see all people as performers all the time. One of the reasons performance is freeing is because it is not based purely on truth or identity. Audiences do not watch James Earl Jones play Othello and question whether he is really the kind of person who could kill his wife, and adults do not demand that young children prove to them that they are really Spider-Man or the Little Mermaid. Instead people take a creative journey with them and allow their performances to impact on them and us. If we look at all human activity and see performance, we have a chance to support people to go beyond who they are and how they have learned to behave up to this point, and to create in an ongoing way other ways of relating to themselves, others, and the elements of their surroundings.

It is particularly valuable for teachers to be able to see their students as performers because it helps them to see children as constantly changing, developing, and becoming. There is a strong tendency to see the children you teach as being fixed in time and space. They are who they are—or at least who you got to know back in September. Think about the children in your class this year. It is probably easy to identify who the leaders and the followers are, who is good at listening, and who is a troublemaker. And while there is obviously some value in being able to predict how students will respond, it can also be limiting. It can become a self-fulfilling prophecy and prevent us from offering students opportunities for seeing who they are becoming.

One of the benefits of doing improv in the classroom is that it makes it apparent that everyone is a performer. Everyone is capable of being who they are and who they are not. Imagine if Jessica, who is shy and rarely answers any questions, were to get up during an improv activity and pretend to be a chef in a fancy restaurant, calling out directions and yelling at the waiters. Chances are it would change how you and the class (including Jessica) saw her from that point forward. Seeing people perform in an improv scene or exercise helps you to see the human capacity to perform in all areas of life. It helps you see your students as capable of changing and growing—of being who they are becoming. In Vygotskian terms, it helps to create a Zone of Proximal Development.

WHAT IS AN ENVIRONMENT?

Doing improv in the classroom helps to create a supportive learning environment, that is, one in which students can take risks and make mistakes. Most of us think of environments as something separate from us, as if we are in environments that were created by someone else. We may go to a party and comment on what a festive environment it is, or we may come home and complain about what a stressful environment there is at work. We think and talk about environments as if they have an existence separate from the people, including us, who are creating them. But what does that mean? How can we be "in" an environment? Environments are not like houses that are standing there waiting for us to come back to them. The people who are in them are continuously creating them. A party is festive because the people at the party, including the host, are creating a festive environment. The work environment is stressful because the people working there are doing things that produce stress. The same is the case with classrooms: Teachers and children create the environment in the classroom; it does not exist separate from them. Even within the constraints of current classrooms and curricula, teachers and children can create supportive (more creative and improvisational) learning environments, and seeing everyone as the creators of the environment is an important component.

Improvising together is extremely useful for helping children to develop as environment creators. In order to have a successful improv scene the performers have to continuously create the environment for the scene to take place, because there is no separation between the creating of the environment for the scene and the scene itself. It all takes place all the time. For example, in order to create a scene that ends up being about two brothers who share a room and are fighting over a bicycle, the performers have to create a physical environment (where they are and what is in the room with them), an emotional environment (how they feel about each other), and what is happening at that moment. The improvisers create all the things we normally think of as being part of an already established environment or relationship during the course of the scene. For this reason, improv is a wonderful way to practice environment-building, and it makes it more difficult for children to relate to the classroom as passive participants rather than active creators.

WHAT IS A GROUP?

Whether they are working with small groups or classes of 30 students, teaching workshop-style or "chalk and talk," teaching to the test or engaging in creative play, teachers are always working with groups. And while all classes are groups, current educational models encourage and even demand that teachers have children work collaboratively in small groups and take responsibility for their own learning. But this is easier said than done, as so many teachers are now discovering. Many teachers do not feel that they are skilled at group facilitation and feel overwhelmed and unprepared for the challenges of today's schools: classes of mixed learning styles and grade levels, a variety of cultural backgrounds and emotional needs, lack of positive role models in students' lives, lack of motivation for learning, and the pressure to raise standards.

It is helpful to remember that all human life is lived in one kind of a group or another. The image of Robinson Crusoe alone on a desert island is a myth; we are an inherently social species and we cannot survive in isolation. The difficulties people have working together effectively as a group come in part from the fact that even though we are born and live our lives in groups (families, communities, clubs, nations), most of us, particularly in Western society, are socialized to only see individuals.

In school this means that teachers and students tend to see the class as collections of individuals, and therefore relate to group work as just a more social way for individuals to learn. From this vantage point the job of the teacher is to help individual children to reach their full potential, and the class is merely the context within which individual children learn. However, most teachers know that in addition to being a collection of individuals, classes have a character of their own that cannot be understood by simply putting together the personalities of each individual child. The class, as a unit, can have a bad day or a good day. The class can be wound up or relaxed. The class has moods. In essence, the class has a character that is influenced by and yet distinct from its individual members.

In addition to having their own character, it also turns out that groups can learn. There are those in the field of psychology and education who have begun to realize that it is possible for *the group* to learn and develop and that groups actually have integrity of their own. And it turns out that when groups develop, individuals learn. While there is a tendency to think that people have to choose between the good of the group and the needs of the individual, it turns out that paying attention to what the group needs supports rather than hinders individual learning. Vygotsky's Zone of Proximal Development is once again useful here. In the creation of the ZPD there are greater opportunities for individuals to go beyond their current level of development and stretch to try out new activities. And since people at many different levels of development are part of creating a ZPD, students are able to creatively imitate and learn from one another. In an environment where the group is working well together, individuals can try out new performances, they can help one another learn new skills and information, and they can imitate their more developed peers.

One can see group learning most clearly in settings outside of school. A dance troupe rehearses tirelessly to perfect their timing. A marching band gets better at playing in unison. Football teams practice each play to make sure that every block, handoff, and pass is precisely orchestrated. While individual talent and individual learning are important, it is not enough for any of these types of groups to succeed. A group of very talented individuals is not always the most successful ensemble or team. A group that works well together can accomplish more than the sum of their individual members.

While all groups can learn, some groups are better at learning than others. A class that works well together can become a more powerful learning unit. More work can be accomplished in the course of a day, and individuals are more likely to learn from and with one another. On a basic level, becoming more developed as a group can help students line up more quickly and move from one activity to another with less conflict and wasted time, and a class that knows how to function as a group can take care of itself when the teacher has to work with an individual child.

When a class is working well together there are more resources in the room. In most classrooms it is the teacher who is responsible for creating the learning environment. The teacher tells the class to quiet down when the noise level rises, she keeps track of who is good at math and bad at spelling, and she hands out praise and encouragement. However, when groups are working well together the class can share the responsibility for the learning environment and can call on one another to help the group learn. Under these conditions, children remind one another what the rules are in productive ways, help one another with a difficult math problem, or welcome a new student. When a class makes effective use of all its resources, everybody has something to contribute. The contributions of quiet students, students who are struggling to learn English, and even difficult students become as valued as those of the gifted and funny students because everyone's talents and challenges become the property of the class as a whole.

Schools often overlook the necessity of teaching kids to perform better as a group. While many students gain these skills outside school, in dance classes and on sports teams, these activities are strikingly absent from classrooms, the grouping in which students spend most of their lives. Improv is a great activity for learning to see that you are part of a group. In addition, when students improvise together they learn important group-building skills. Improv is similar to team sports in that everyone is expected to use their skills for the benefit of the ensemble.

This is not an easy task. So much of life (and school in particular) is about looking good, being a star, or, if that is not possible, trying to fade into the woodwork. In improv, if a scene is going to be successful, everyone has to take responsibility for the group's success (and no one person can be blamed for its failure). Like team sports, when an improv troupe is working well together everyone is there for each other—they have one another's backs. Imagine how much learning could happen in the classroom if the class related to one another this way—as partners in the learning process.

TEACHERS AS IMPROVISERS

We've talked about the benefits for children's learning and for the class as a whole, but what about teachers? It turns out that learning to improvise can be very helpful for teachers as well. Researchers have found that the difference between novice and experienced teachers is the extent to which they improvise. Experienced and skilled teachers may start with a plan of what the class is going to do, but in the course of a lesson they are able to diverge from that plan and go in a different direction if something new emerges. Experienced teachers think on their feet. While they may come in with a plan or an objective, they are able and willing to change what they are doing based on what the students do or say. They are impacted by their students' curiosity or confusion.

Learning to improvise in the theatrical sense provides teachers with tools that can improve their practice. By learning to see their class as an ensemble and themselves as a member (sometimes) and a director (at other times) of that ensemble, teachers can start to recognize, accept, and say, "Yes, and" to their students' offers. Research on teaching has shown that the more teachers can respond to what children are offering, the more they can use everything that is said and done, the better teachers they become. They are no longer distracted by interruptions, questions, or mistakes. In theatrical language, these offers become the material for the ongoing classroom play.

However, improvising can also be challenging for teachers. They have to be willing to go on a creative journey with children without knowing what is going to happen. Teachers are often nervous about improvising. They themselves have been through years of schooling that all too often train them to stop being improvisational. Not surprisingly, by the time people become teachers they have lost some of the skills they need to be a good improviser: the willingness to look silly or foolish, to not know what is going to happen next, to do what you don't know how to do. Because of this, the children are often better at improv than teachers and this can feel threatening.

The bottom line is that improvising with children will probably require teachers to learn and develop—to do what they don't know how to do, to be who they are (a competent adult and teacher) and who they are not (a theatrical improviser). While this may feel a little scary, it is also invaluable in creating a supportive learning environment. What better example can teachers set for the children they work with than that we are going on the journey alongside them?

As we have said throughout this chapter, all human beings are performers and life is improvisational. One of the values, therefore, of learning to improvise in the theatrical sense is that it can help people to develop all of their life performances, including the performance of being a teacher or a student. While the rest of this book is focused on improv as a theatrical activity, we urge you to always keep in mind the ways in which you and your students are always performing together and think about how what you are learning can be of use to you and your students everywhere.

Chapter 2

What Is Improv? How Do You Do It?

The purpose of this chapter is to help you get started using improv in the classroom. We begin with the basic principles of improvisation, the foundation on which all the activities in this book are built. This section includes the directions for "Yes, and," the most basic and important game that improvisers learn, which teaches these principles. We then give some guidelines on how to introduce and use improv in an elementary or middle school classroom, including when to play, where to play, how to explain the games to children, and how to respond to various situations that might come up during and after the activities. We have also included a glossary of improv terms for use in the classroom.

THE BASIC PRINCIPLES OF IMPROV

Improvisers follow a set of guiding principles that help them work together. In addition to being the starting point for all of the improv activities in this book, these principles are also useful for transforming the performance of classroom life and other life activities. These principles include:

- The giving and receiving of offers
- Don't negate
- Make the ensemble look good
- "Yes, and"

These principles, as important as they are, are not meant to be mastered before participants can play the game; they are, in our opinion, never mastered, but are constantly practiced. In this way, doing improv is more like going to the gym than it is like learning to ride a bicycle. Once we have learned to ride a bicycle it becomes something we know how to do. Whether we continue riding or not, we know how to ride. However, while we get stronger the more we work out at the gym, we never reach a point where we can say, "I have mastered being in shape; I don't have to work out anymore." Even very experienced improvisers find ways to practice the principles of improv because it helps keep their improv muscles in shape. As students learn and practice these principles they will be able to work together more effectively, get more enjoyment out of the activities, and create more and more engaging scenes.

The Giving and Receiving of Offers

The basic unit of improv is the offer. Everything that any participant says or does in a scene is an offer. They can be movements, sounds, words, or ideas. Improv scenes are created by the giving and receiving of those offers. For example, if one improviser gets up onstage and shrugs her shoulders, that shrug is an offer and is now available for the ensemble to use. Another improviser might respond by saying, "I'll help you get that monster off your back."

The job of the improv ensemble is to get better and better at seeing and building with offers. This is not easy; for one thing, there is a tendency to only accept the offers that one likes or is comfortable with and to think that all others are not really offers. For example, in an activity where the group is sending a sound and a movement around the circle (e.g., "Sound Ball,") someone might make a burping sound. Whether or not the other members of the ensemble like that offer is not the point; it is still an offer. When an improv performance isn't working, you can bet that the improvisers aren't seeing offers or are ignoring the ones they see. Skilled improvisers can see the offer in anything.

Here are some examples of offers and one way they might be accepted and used by a second improviser (remember, it's improv—there are also an infinite number of ways they could be accepted):

Performer 1: (Shrugs her shoulders)
Performer 2: You might not care if you fail math, young lady, but I do.

Performer 1: (Pointing up) Look!
Performer 2: (Looking around) I knew Spider-Man would save us.

Performer 1: What happened to your hair?
Performer 2: My baby brother didn't like his peas, so he decided to throw them at me. What a mess!

The best performers don't just accept offers, they celebrate them, as though the suggestion that they crawl on the ground like turtles was the most exciting idea they had ever heard. They don't simply see offers, they build with them enthusiastically.

Negation

When improvisers do not accept an offer it is called a negation, and as any improviser will tell you, the rule in improv is *don't negate*. Negating, or blocking, is challenging, disagreeing with, or otherwise denying the reality of what has been presented so far in the scene. So if your fellow performer asks you to help lift an elephant off his legs, one example of a negation would be to say, "There's no elephant on your legs."

Beginning improvisers may want to stay away from negative words such as *no, not,* and *isn't.* But be careful: Blocking an offer doesn't always involve these dangerous little words, and saying yes does not always prevent a negation. One of the most common forms of negation is when improvisers say "Yes, but" to one another's offers. This does not mean there isn't disagreement in improv, but characters who want to disagree must work hard to include the offers that have come before in the disagreement. For example, in a scene where students are performing on a talk show as George Washington and King George III of England, King George would probably disagree with Washington's complaints about taxation without representation. However, it would be a negation for him to say, "I didn't tax you." Here are some more examples of negations:

Performer 1: Let's pack up the car and head to the beach.
Performer 2: There's no beach around here.

Performer 1: [Says nothing, and mimes throwing a very large heavy object toward her partner.]
Performer 2: [Puts out one hand and "catches" the object easily.]

Performer 1: I love you so much, let's get married.
Performer 2: I've never seen you before in my life.

Performer 1: My brother is stronger than your brother.
Performer 2: Yes, but he's not really as strong as you think he is.

While negation may get a laugh from the audience, it also stalls the action and keeps the scene from moving forward. It often leaves some performers out of the scene, thus giving the ensemble less to create with. Working to accept and build with offers, regardless of how silly, confusing, or unwanted they are, ensures that the ensemble has material to build with.

In our experience, negation does not only occur in improv scenes. Human beings block each other's offers all the time. For example, if a student walks up to a teacher and says, "I have to go to the bathroom," an understandable, but negating, response might be, "No, you don't. You just went 15 minutes ago." While there might be a reason why the teacher does not want the student to return to the bathroom, denying that she has to go at all is a negation. Inevitably, students (and teachers) will block heavily in improv scenes they do together, just as they are likely to do in all areas of classroom life. Saying no actively or by ignoring what has been said is a common occurrence; however, learning to avoid negation in improv, and in life, can help groups of students and teachers develop skills for creating a more inclusive learning environment.

Make the Ensemble Look Good

Professional improvisers often say, "Your partner is a genius." Being funny and talented in improv is actually about making the ensemble look good. Just as in team sports, improvisers work at "having one another's backs." For example, if the ensemble is making up a collective story and one improviser stutters instead of saying a sentence, the next improviser might say, "Billy saw a ghost and could barely speak." While improvisers trust that their fellow performers will pick up and nurture their offers, they also recognize that they have a responsibility to make offers that are of use to the ensemble.

"Yes, and"

Successful improv is more than just seeing or accepting offers. In order for the activity to develop, the ensemble has to add to the offers that have already been made. In improv, building on offers is called "Yes, and." If players accept one another's offers but don't add any new action or information, the improv activity will not develop beyond its starting point. With "Yes, and," an improviser goes beyond what is offered and adds something new. For example,

> *Performer 1:* It sure is hot here on the moon.
> *Performer 2:* Let's hike over to the dark side and see if we can find some shade.
> *Performer 1:* OK, bring the ray gun. I'm not going to let the giant slime creature eat another one of my crew.

In this three-line exchange the players have used each line to move the scene along by providing more information for the further development of the scene. While "Yes, and" is critical to successful improv, it is important to add lines in such a way that the offers that came before are not blocked, ignored, or leapt over. Here are some examples of successful "Yes, and" offers:

> *Performer 1:* Have you seen the doctor about the lump on your head?
> *Performer 2:* Yeah, she gave me some cream to rub on it every day.

> *Performer 1:* I have to go to the bathroom.
> *Performer 2:* Are you OK? It's only been 15 minutes since you went last time.
> *Performer 1:* Well, I did drink three cups of juice at lunch.

What's important in these exchanges is that the offer is accepted *and* something has been added to further the scene that the other characters and you can now continue to build with.

Professional improvisers on television or at a comedy club are basically doing "Yes, and" all the time. Because the skill of "Yes, and" incorporates the giving and receiving of offers, the avoidance of negating or blocking, and the skill of adding something to the scene, even highly trained improvisers practice it frequently. One tool improvisors use to practice is a storytelling variation of "Yes, and" called "Yes, and Collective Story" where the participants make up a story as if they are one person—they tell it in one voice. Each person has a sentence and each sentence begins with the words "Yes, and." The "yes" signifies that the person accepts and has heard everything that came before—not only what the person right before him or her said, but everything that has been said in the story so far. The "yes" requires that each person be very attentive and focused and accept everything that is said as real. The "and" directs each person to add a little something to the story.

We have included the directions for a "Yes, and" activity on page 18 to illuminate the improv fundamentals and to provide an introduction to how to teach the games in this book, as well as to introduce how we have formatted them in subsequent chapters. The version of "Yes, and" on page 18 is only one of several variations included in this book. In particular, Chapter 4 features this activity with many variations. Though it can be challenging, you will want to play it frequently with your students.

While it might be good to review or discuss the fundamentals of improv before teaching this game, keep in mind that mistakes can be turned into offers. No amount of preparation will keep students from negating, for example, but as the game is played these moments can be highlighted to provide students with an opportunity to reflect as they go. Remind your students that improv is a "doing" activity; you are not expecting them to "get it" or "master it." Mistakes can always be used to continue to build the ensemble. Let them know that you will be interrupting them so that the class can continue to learn from the choices they make.

IMPROVISING A STAGE AND PROPS

Understandably, most people think of a stage as a raised platform at the front of an auditorium. It's often thought of as the only place in which pretending and performance can take place. But just as learning can (and does) take place anywhere, so can any location become a place for performance. Think about children in the hallway before class, or on the playground. They are always performing. Children can perform everywhere: waiting in line for the bathroom, on the bus heading to a field trip, or with everyone sitting at their seats. While it is possible to perform anywhere, there is also a value in designating a particular spot as a stage, either temporarily or permanently. When students step into that space, they are given permission to be something other than who they are—to consciously perform.

Improvisational activities are widely varied with regard to their physical demands. Some activities can be done seated in a circle, others can be done riding on the bus or walking to music class, while still others may best be done on the playground or in the gym. However, don't allow restrictions such as a cramped space or desks bolted to the floor keep you from trying new games. Sometimes the best improvisational moments come out of the creativity required when dealing with a limited space. Many activities in this book can be done with students seated at their desks or with a few chairs placed in the front of the classroom.

"Yes, and" Collective Story

Improv Level: Beginner

Grade Level: All

Time Needed: 30–40 minutes

Materials: None

This activity teaches the vital improvisational skill of accepting offers. When students are able to suspend their impulse to shape the story to match their own desired outcome, they will be amazed at what they collectively create. It is likely that this game will take several attempts to master, and it never ceases to be challenging.

Directions

The class sits in a circle. The teacher explains that they are going to tell a story together. Each person will contribute one sentence and everyone (except the first person) will start their sentence with the words "Yes, and." The story should be told in the third person (avoid *I, me, we, us*). The teacher solicits suggestions for a title from the class. The teacher then repeats the title and begins the story by saying the first sentence. The person to the teacher's right continues the story, starting his or her sentence with the words "Yes, and" and adding a sentence. The story proceeds with each consecutive person adding one sentence beginning with "Yes, and" to the story. Students should be encouraged not to try to move the story along too quickly or to steer it in their own direction, but instead to build gradually on what has been said. A successful story might not "go" very far but might still be very satisfying. The story ends whenever the teacher feels it has reached a conclusion, or time has run out.

Hints

- The first few times you do this activity the teacher should say the first line. Model a good first line by making sure to include "who" the story is about, "where" it takes place, and a little bit of action. For example, "Johnny woke up, looked out his window, and began to cry."
- Avoid using the names of people in the room.
- This activity can be very challenging for students who want to shape the story or make a bold or silly offer. Consider stopping students when they do this and reminding them to attend to what was said previously.

Side Coaching

- "How might you *use the offer* you just got from (name of person who just spoke before)?"
- "Add a line that *could not* have been said without the line before it."
- "What's the *very next* thing that happened in the story?"
- "Let the group tell the story."

Extension

- There are many extensions to "Yes, and" available throughout the book, particularly in Chapter 4.

For many games, you will want to have either an open space where children can sit in a circle, either in chairs or on the floor, or a theater-style space with a small performance area in front facing an audience area. For the former, a classroom rug will often suffice, though teachers may wish to push surrounding furniture back to allow more room for movement. A theater-style space can be quickly arranged on the rug, with taller students sitting in back, or alternatively, students' desks can form the audience with performers coming to the front of the room where the teacher stands. Wherever you choose to improvise, work with your students to make the space you designate as a stage, however crude or temporary, into a special, respected place.

In improvisation, props are any item such as a chair or a ball that are helpful in creating a scene or playing a game, and in improv they are generally kept to a minimum. Skilled improvisers can fashion an imaginary prop out of anything or, better yet, invent the object altogether by miming it in the action. Students should be discouraged from scouring the classroom to find objects to add to their scenes. These may distract from the action and limit their creativity. Remind students that a key component of improv is imagination. When actual props are necessary to make a scene work, we've listed them in the headings for each activity. Aside from chairs, a soft, easy-to-catch ball and a bell are common improv props that would be useful to have on hand.

CHOOSING THE ACTIVITIES

The activities included in this book can be done at many different times of the day. All of them can be done during a designated improv time that can happen once a day or once a week, depending on your schedule. This book also includes activities that are valuable for teaching curriculum content, whether it be social studies, science, reading, or math. These activities can easily be integrated into the other learning activities for those subjects. Finally, many of the shorter activities can be used during transitions, both inside the classroom and while moving to and from activities elsewhere in school.

This book is organized to help you select activities for all of these times, but don't be limited by our categories: If you find an ensemble game that would work well with a math lesson, use it. And once you're comfortable with the procedures for a given activity, change them around and encourage your students to offer suggestions to make it their own. As you play together, the class will discover old favorites, the playing of which can become part of the culture of the class.

When you do choose to set aside a block of time in your schedule for improv, your class will have a chance to immerse itself in the material and to learn the basics, hone their improvisational technique, and reflect on how they are working together at building their ensemble and creating their learning environment. Consider starting or ending the week with a dedicated improv session, or making a few improv games a part of every day's morning meeting or afternoon-dismissal routine. These periods can be an opportunity for your class to practice and rehearse as they form an improv troupe.

It is a good idea to begin an improv session with a warmup activity. These activities, which are usually whole-group circle games, allow the class to transition into a playful, improvisational mode. Many of the games in Chapter 3 can be used as excellent activities for transitions. When preparing to do improv, consider the physical, emotional, and social demands of the activities. The culture of improvisation is sometimes different from other classroom activities (like a math lesson), so exercises that help students remember that they are working as an ensemble are useful to include earlier in a lesson. Finally, keep the energy demands of the activities under consideration. An activity that involves a lot of movement or loud noise can be followed with another that will help lower the tone.

THE AUDIENCE PERFORMANCE

While some of the activities in this book are designed for everyone to participate at once, many require that just a few students perform while the rest of the class is in the audience. Even when they are in the audience, however, students should be reminded that they are still part of the performance.

Early in the process of introducing improvisation to a class, take the time to teach students about the demands of this very important role. Ask them what they think the audience member characters might look like. How might they sound? What props do they need? How is their role in the scene important? Take time to practice various performances as a group. Encourage students to laugh when the performance is funny, cry when it's sad, and, above all, applaud with joy when their fellow classmates perform onstage. As students rehearse their audience performances, give them characters to practice. For example, have them perform as elephants watching ballet or as grandparents at a kindergarten graduation.

As with learning any new skill, learning to perform can be challenging. There will be plenty of times when students perform scenes or attempt activities and they don't quite work. It is still important in these moments to perform as an enthusiastic audience. Responses like applause are ways of praising and supporting the performers for their work, not an evaluation of the performance. You might even want to consciously play with some more negative audience performances where the class boos, talks among themselves, or makes negative comments. This can lead to some very interesting discussions about how these types of audience performances can make it difficult for the people onstage to do their job.

For the first few times that you try scene work with your class, in your capacity as the director, make a point of introducing each character to the scene with enthusiasm, modeling for the audience how to applaud while each actor comes onstage. As much as possible, play the part of the gracious, eager emcee who sets the tone for the performance. When students are more confident, invite one of them to take over the role of emcee for a day, introducing each scene, performer, and character to the audience and leading them in creating a supportive environment where everyone can take risks.

WHO'S IN CHARGE OF SAFETY?

While improv is a creative activity that can get silly at times, it does not follow that children can do whatever they want, regardless of the consequences. It's a good idea to reinforce that the rules already established in your classroom about physical and emotional safety should remain the same, and it may be valuable to remind students that while some rules have changed, certain behaviors, as always, are not allowed. For example, be clear about the difference between performing fighting and actually fighting. No matter what they are doing together, performers are always taking care of the ensemble, whether in taking care to accept and further offers or protecting one another from harm.

INTRODUCING THE ACTIVITIES

As with any new activity, it is a good idea to introduce new improv games or scenes one at a time and to review them each time they are played. It is almost always appropriate and useful to demonstrate a new activity. Besides helping children understand what they are supposed to do, it makes it clear that you are not asking them to do anything you are not willing to do yourself. One way to demonstrate a new activity is to teach it to one or two children prior to introducing it to the whole class and then ask those children to help you demonstrate it for the rest of the class.

When introducing an activity, avoid the tendency to overteach the rules ahead of time. As we keep saying, improv is learned through doing; it is an activity, and the children will develop their improv muscles through playing, not by listening to you describe the game.

Hints

All of the activities have a set of step-by-step directions for how to play the game or set up the scene. In addition, for many of the activities we have included several additional hints that can help you better understand the activity.

Side Coaching

Side coaching is making suggestions to performers or, more appropriately, to an ensemble while the scene is taking place, much like a soccer coach directing his players from the sidelines. Included in the description of most games is a list of side coaching prompts. Side coaching is not intended as a strategy for "getting it right," but rather as a means for helping performers see and build with offers that they may be missing and for supporting them when they get stuck.

Extensions

Extensions are suggestions for how each game might be adapted for another use, such as with a new academic subject, or made more challenging once students have mastered its basic setup. As you become more familiar with the activities, allow the extensions to serve as inspiration for you and your students as you come up with your own ways of adapting and extending each activity.

The Debrief

Following a performance, an ensemble will commonly gather to discuss what worked and did not work in a production. They provide an excellent opportunity to explore improv fundamentals, to establish class norms for working together, and to give direction to future exercises the class may do together. One way of thinking about a debrief is as a kind of ensemble meeting where the class can reflect on its performance and make decisions about how they want to continue to work together. You might ask students what they saw in the scene. What offers did they notice? At what points do they think they could have done a better job building on one another's offers?

The debrief, like side coaching, is not about critiquing or "fixing" mistakes but is rather an ongoing discussion through which the class continually creates its collective development as an ensemble. Just as during scenes and activities, suggestions and comments made in the debrief are offers and should be related to as such by all participants. Use the rules of improv to guide your discussions as you create an environment where mistakes are related to in this new way.

BRINGING THE SKILLS AND LANGUAGE OF IMPROV INTO (THE REST OF) THE CLASSROOM

As you and your students become more skilled at improvising together, there will be inevitable moments throughout the day when you will all be reminded of something you have worked on while improvising. Perhaps someone will lose focus and drop the ball while reading a story out loud. At other times, you may catch yourself saying the words "no, but" and then suggest you and the class "try that scene again." We strongly encourage both spontaneous and more intentional efforts to bring the language of improvisation into all of your classroom interactions (and beyond!). Cleanup time, for example, could become "strike," the term an acting company uses for the time following a production when the scenery is taken apart and the stage is restored to its preshow conditions. Students and teachers alike can "take two," as in the above example. Opportunities to discuss the giving and receiving of (or failure to give or receive) offers are plentiful.

As we said in Chapter 1, we believe that human beings are performers and that people are performing all the time. From this perspective, there is no limit to the usefulness of improvisational language in transforming how a class interacts, and a conscious attempt to integrate this terminology can serve as a continuous reminder that people are always making performance choices. A glossary of improvisational terms is included at the end of this chapter and may serve as a guide in this endeavor.

ASSESSMENT

Understandably, inventive teachers venturing to bring something new into their classrooms will want a mechanism for evaluating the success of such an endeavor. In addition to a desire to advance their practice as teachers and therefore impact on student learning, teachers choosing to integrate improv into their curricula will undoubtedly need to field questions from administrators, colleagues, parents, and students themselves about the efficacy of such an approach as well as a benchmark for rating students' individual and collective progress. In short, in a world concerned with grades and outcome measures, how does one evaluate a program without compromising its uniqueness as a mistake-free activity that is continuously created by its participants?

Not surprisingly, we do not recommend giving grades or otherwise singling out individual student performances. Rather, it is important to be mindful that the class succeeds or fails in improv as a group. It is our contention that introducing improv into a class can and will help students become, first and foremost, better learners. Success, in this regard, should be evident in students' development in the fundamentals of improvisation both while improvising formally and in all of their interactions in the classroom. How are students doing at making use of offers and avoiding negation in their academic and informal conversations in the classroom? Are they using the language of improvisation in other contexts? Are they listening to one another and to you in order to hear and build with offers? Do participants respond during classroom discussions or other learning times in ways that are mindful of an obligation not just to get the right answer but to contribute to the group's learning as a whole?

There are no set mechanisms for evaluating these critical questions. Evaluation of improv works best as an ongoing activity done with the class. Debriefs and other conversations about improv provide a conceptual framework for approaching this. Success can be considered performatory, with students creating improvised scenes designed to illustrate what they have learned from their work doing improv together. Administrators, parents, and colleagues can be invited to observe or, better yet, participate in demonstrations of what has been learned. This may provide the best evidence for what has been produced.

INCLUDING EVERYONE IN IMPROV

Improvisation is fundamentally an inclusive activity that can actually help to make a classroom more fully accessible to students with different needs. In improv, all performers have a responsibility for the success of the scene, whether they are seasoned performers or novices. Everyone's contributions, in the form of offers, are made use of to build the scene. Imagine the implications for an inclusive classroom. The offers made by children with minimal English skills or those with designated learning disabilities are as much offers as any other. The question in improv is always "How can we create this scene, given what we collectively have to give?"

Shy or Reticent Children

Particularly early on, some students may feel reluctant to participate in the improv activities. Perhaps they are shy, intimidated by the thought of performance, or reluctant to risk "making a mistake" in front of the class. We believe that improv should be a voluntary activity. There is nothing that turns something playful into a chore more than being forced to participate. If children do not want to play the game, they can always perform as an audience member.

It is useful to relate to nonparticipation (and even participation that may interfere with the activities themselves) not as a nonperformance (or counterperformance), but as a performance in itself. Students who choose not to come onstage still have an obligation to perform their role as a member of the audience. These students may also be cast in roles with specific responsibilities such as a timekeeper or a designated observer in charge of taking note of how well the class is building on offers, for example. Moments when these students are engaged, laugh, or briefly join in can be capitalized on by a responsive teacher who is quick to recognize them as offers that may be made use of as part of the class's collective performance.

Children with Special Needs

Improvisational activities can accommodate students with all kinds of disabilities. Some modifications will be minor. You need to allow extra room for children to move when improvising with students who use a wheelchair. Having a child who is hearing-impaired will require carefully picking and choosing the activities that work for your students. Just as with any other learning space in the classroom, the stage should be fully accessible to all students.

Students can participate in improv in a variety of ways. One effective strategy for helping a student who has difficulty grasping material involved in a scene or who is reluctant to perform is to make that student an assistant director. Involve him or her in planning the lesson and allow input on strategies in a sort of preproduction meeting. Not only does this give that student a sense of responsibility and ownership, it provides a nonthreatening context for previewing written material and preparing that student for the demands of a scene.

Some students may require a designated assistant for some activities. This may be their regular classroom aid, an assistant teacher, or another student. Be creative in your use of these extra players. Include them in the action, or make use of theatrical techniques to relate to their presence as an offer. For example, students with difficulty speaking might mime their performance while someone else dubs the words from offstage or from another part of the scene. Perhaps a child in need of assistance and an aide can act as one two-headed character or join together with the aide positioned behind with arms underneath so that the student provides the words and the aide the hand movements.

In improv, things that might be considered a disruption during other activities can be incorporated into the activity in a new way. For example, a student who is always calling out or making silly noises can be the star of a game like "Sound Ball" or "Shout It Out" where blurting out ridiculous sounds is a key to the activity. There is enough variety and flavor in improv to allow for anyone's strengths to be made use of. Improv allows for opportunities for what is ordinarily a difficulty to become highlighted and used to help the ensemble grow.

GLOSSARY OF IMPROVISATIONAL TERMS

Improvisation and theater, like any discipline, have their own set of unique terms as well as familiar words that are used in new ways. Familiarizing yourself with the basic vocabulary of improv will allow you to better understand the activities in this book, enjoy watching improv, and use the terms when side coaching or debriefing with your students. As we discussed earlier, once students are familiar with the concepts outlined here, you can use them at other times of the day. Imagine telling the class they need to clean up as an ensemble or suggesting to a student during morning meeting that she accept an offer given by another student.

Accepting an Offer: Saying yes to something one's partner suggests or gives in a scene; embracing and using the unexpected.

Action: The activity of the scene; the director (either the teacher or a designated student) indicates that the scene is to begin by yelling "Action!"

Call and Response: Any activity where a leader calls out and the group responds by repeating in unison what was called. In a call-and-response activity, students may take turns being the leader.

Character: A role taken on by an actor during a scene or play that includes physical, vocal, and affective components of that role; staying in character means maintaining the pretense of being in that role. Students should be encouraged not to step out of character by addressing a scene partner or the class as themselves in the middle of a scene.

Cut: The scene's director shouts "Cut!" to end a scene or activity. Other terms that can be used to end scenes are "Curtain" or "Thank you."

Energy: An invisible force that can be created, shaped, and shared among actors; the degree of intensity of a performance.

Ensemble: The collective players in a group, scene, or class who work together to achieve some end; the audience for any improvisational activity may be considered part of an ensemble.

Entrance: Any time a new performer enters a scene; performers should enter in character.

Focus: Directing attention on a particular person or object; individual performers may have distinct foci, or the ensemble may share a focus.

Freeze: The director may shout "Freeze!" to pause all movement and vocalization in an activity, or may call "Freeze!" in order to give direction to the characters; unlike "Cut," *freeze* indicates that the action will resume after a brief pause for redirection or reflection.

Longform: A style of improvisation where the performers create a full-length play by improvising a series of interconnected scenes.

Making an Offer: Presenting an idea, thought, movement, or activity to one's partner or to the ensemble; considered to be a sign of a talented improviser.

"No, but": The opposite of "yes, and"; when a performer says, "no, but," whether she says the words or not, she is negating an offer.

Platform: Establishing the *who* (relationship), *what* (action), and *where* (location) of the scene, key to moving a scene forward; improvisers work to establish these elements as early as possible in a scene.

Props: Any object used in a performance such as a hairbrush or a chair; in improvisation props are usually imaginary.

Recognizing an Offer: Distinguishing the element, positive or negative, in another's performance on which one can build.

Relationship: The circumstances that connect any two or more people; the reason they are together in the scene.

Role: The part one plays in a scene or elsewhere in life that carries with it a subscribed set of rules and conditions governing the performance choices allowable within it.

Scene: A dramatic space in which a staged performance takes place.

Scene Partner(s): The improvisers performing in the scene.

Set Pieces: Elements in a performance space that cannot be easily moved.

Side Coaching: The arrangement during a scene where the director or a fellow actor provides support and ideas from outside the scene to a player in the scene.

Stage: Any environment where a performance takes place; a stage can be a classroom, the hallway, or the playground. As Shakespeare said, "All the world's a stage."

Strike: Taking apart a set after a performance; traditionally the entire cast and company helps out with the strike. In improv, the strike may consist of rearranging furniture and putting away props.

"Yes, and": The fundamental activity of improvisation. Saying "yes" (literally or otherwise) means hearing and accepting everything that has come before in the scene. Saying "and" means you add something to it to further the dialogue or the action.

Chapter 3

Creating the Ensemble

A class that works well together as a group can learn more. While many students learn to work in groups outside of school, informally on the playground, and more formally in dance classes and on sports teams, these activities are typically absent from classrooms, the grouping in which students spend most of their lives. While all of improv is about the ensemble, there are some activities that are specifically designed to help create an ensemble and can be used to teach children some of the skills that help an ensemble (in this case, the class) work well together. This chapter contains activities that are designed to help create the improv ensemble and, in turn, help support your class to work together more collaboratively.

Learning to improvise together helps teachers and students to see that the class is a group and that they are part of that group. As students explore the activities in this chapter, they will begin to develop an awareness of their class as a unique social unit. Students can start to see themselves, their class, and learning itself in a new way, as socially created. In time, students create, through improvisation, a shared culture and language that can positively impact the rest of their work in the classroom.

When a group is working well together, individuals can learn more. While this may seem paradoxical, think about what happens when a group is cooperating and collaborating. The group doesn't get bogged down in transitions, in judging who is doing well and who isn't, or in arguing over who did what to whom. Teachers are more able to tend to the specific needs of individual students when they are confident that the class as a whole can work well together. The simplest activities in this chapter, such as "Sound Ball," "Woosh!," and "Zip! Zap! Zop!," ask only that students work as a coordinated group. These games require the whole group to focus on successfully passing an imaginary ball or sound around the circle. If they take their eye off the group, the ball is dropped or the clap does not make it around the circle. The excitement students experience comes from completing the activity together.

When improvising together, the challenge to the class is to make use of the offers the group receives, while at the same time working to have every offer be given with the interest of the group in mind. It is in this sense that in improv anything is possible and yet it is not "anything goes." As students learn to improvise, they must continually negotiate accepting offers while at the same time making sure that offers are made on behalf of the group. Working together as a group does not mean that different individuals do not make different contributions; when a group is performing at its best, everyone is challenged to contribute everything they have to give. Activities such as "Make a Machine," "Yes, Let's," and "What Are You Doing?" support children to make their unique offers as part of a collective endeavor.

Because everything is an offer, the difficulties that individuals have are not obstacles to the group's success but become material for the group to create with. In improvisational scenes the contributions of every child are treated as valuable offers and the "oddball," the "new kid," the "slow kid," the "troublemaker," and the "smart aleck" are recast in the context of the scene. In none of the activities are students allowed to vote the "weakest link" out of the game. More advanced activities such as "Still Life" and "Remote Control" give children a chance to work with one another to create a scene where the success of that scene is dependent on all offers being used.

DEVELOPING GROUP-BUILDING SKILLS

When improvising together, students are continually asked, in a variety of ways, "How are we going to do this together? How can we do this better?" In this sense, improvisers are challenged to grow collectively. In "Counting, How High?" and "Pass the Pulse" the group has to work together in order to reach a goal. In a sense, the class competes with itself to do a bit better than the last time. The members of the class become better improvisers by working at it together.

Improvisation is a great opportunity to develop students' skills at leading and following. One way for a group to function well together is to designate and follow a leader. In order to do this, everyone needs to agree that, for the moment, one person is the leader, and to follow his or her leadership. Classes that are able to do this are better able to function together. Activities such as "Mirrors" and "Group Sculpture" provide opportunities for children to explore and develop their skills at performing as leaders and followers and switching between the two.

Other activities in this chapter, such as "Maah" and "My Song, Our Song," require that the group literally speak with one voice. To do so, students must supplant their impulse to be a star and suspend their urge to shape the scene. This brings into the classroom the experience of a choir or a marching band. Students learn that they can create something beautiful (or funny, or strange, or smart) together.

As students work to advance their improv skills, they will need to discover more advanced ways of being supportive of one another. While students naturally tend to offer help to one another, particularly when they see the possibility of accomplishing more, they are often underdeveloped in their skill at doing so. For example, in an attempt to

be helpful a student may call out the answer to a math problem, sup-
planting the opportunity for other students to try to find the answer on
their own. In other moments, students may be so caught up in telling
their classmates to quiet down that their requests become disruptions
themselves. Often these interventions can be poorly timed or even hurt-
ful. In improv, helping another student (reminding them of the rules,
teaching them a particular skill) must always be done on behalf of the
ensemble. Through improvising together, students can learn that letting
go of a concern for what other students are doing in place of a concern
for the group as a whole is often most successful.

DEVELOPING EMOTIONALLY

A critical part of creating the ensemble in the classroom involves supporting children to develop emotionally. School is an emotional experience (as is all of life). Many children come to school unprepared to
handle the emotions that arise while working and playing with other
people. For the most part, however, schools are focused on learning as a
primarily cognitive, and not an emotional, activity. Emotions are related
to as something that can get in the way of learning rather than as an
ever-present part of learning. This results in a situation where emotions
are not used in the service of learning.

Improv provides an opportunity to develop new emotions and new
emotional responses; it gives children the experience of the infinite ways
in which one can respond to any given situation. In improv, emotions
are some of the most important resources for the development of scenes.
Rather than being scripted, emotions are something people can create
and something to be created with. Improvisers are constantly expanding
their emotional repertoire, including creating new emotions.

During improv activities, children can break out of the stereotype of
who can be emotional in what ways. Macho boys can perform sad, and
quiet girls can perform angry. Improv allows children to try on different
emotional responses: One does not always have to respond with anger
when someone steps on your foot; sometimes it is more helpful to laugh
or cry or burst into song. Children can even perform emotions they have
never heard of before or put together emotions that do not usually go
together. For example, in "Emotional Mélange," students play with what
it would be like to be happy/sad or jealous/curious. In activities like
"Emotional Bus" and "Emotional Orchestra," children have the experience of performing many different emotions in big and small ways.

From a very young age people can get stuck in emotional ruts that
get in the way of learning and development. Learning to expand their
emotional repertoire gives children more choices. In the classroom this
means that emotions become one of the resources available for creating the ensemble and thus the environment for learning. Rather than

having knee-jerk emotional reactions to other people and to learning, children and teachers can be creative in their responses and can learn to contribute their emotions for the further development of the learning environment.

SETUP OF THE CHAPTER

The activities described in this chapter range from the simplest of circle games to activities that begin to introduce students to improvisational scene work. While they are all focused on ensemble-building, we have also provided extension activities that can be used to introduce and practice subject area concepts. The activities in this chapter are designed to help the class develop as an ensemble—by helping students to create and maintain a focus on the group, and by teaching the class how to listen for and accept offers, speak with one voice, and explore their emotionality. These skills will serve the class well as you continue to explore the other improv activities in this book, and will help your class work more effectively, supportively, and creatively during all classroom activities.

After you and your students have learned these activities and played them several times, you might refer to them at other times of the day. Try reminding students of what worked while playing these games. For example, before discussing a guided reading story, you might suggest that the group do it as if they were playing "Counting, How High?," with everyone being aware of talking one at a time and of supporting the group's discussion rather than trying to be a star. As you start to use ensemble talk throughout the day, your students might even begin to remind themselves to say, "Yes, let's" rather than "No way."

Activities on Working in Unison

This first group of activities involves working in unison with your fellow performers to create a collective performance. Some of them, for example, "Mirrors," give students the intimate experience of being completely in sync with another person or with the whole class. These activities teach students the importance of paying careful attention to their partner or partners so that they can create something together. Students will develop their skills at watching and listening as they learn to "keep their eyes on the group."

Sound Ball

Improv Level: Beginner

Grade Level: All

Time Needed: 10–15 minutes (less once everyone knows the game)

Materials: None

"Sound Ball" is a great way to start improvising—it's fun, simple, and allows everybody to make creative offers. In "Sound Ball," students learn how to work together as a coordinated group by giving and receiving the most basic of offers (a sound and a movement). Students are given an opportunity to act before thinking, a pleasant respite for those who struggle to censor themselves in other classroom activities.

Directions

Everyone stands in a circle. The teacher begins by making eye contact with a student across the circle and tossing an imaginary ball to that student with an accompanying silly sound. For example, the teacher might throw a very large, heavy ball and make the sound "oooomph" as she throws it. The student accepts the offer by "catching" the same-size imaginary ball and by repeating the sound. The student then makes eye contact with another student and passes the ball on with a new sound.

Hints

- When introducing the "ball" to the group, demonstrate its weight, size, and texture. In the language of improv, "endow" the ball for the group; make it seem real. Explain that the ball is an important object and you would not want to see it dropped or damaged.
- It's usually not necessary to make sure that everyone gets a turn. Worrying about turns takes the focus off of the ensemble. Remind the students that they should quickly pass the "ball" and not think too much about who they are passing it to. This will usually ensure that everyone gets a turn.

Side Coaching

- "What could we do to make the ball seem more real?"
- "Don't think before you make your noise."
- "Keep the ball moving."
- If students are still moving too slowly: "Imagine the ball is incredibly hot; don't burn yourself."
- "Make eye contact before you 'throw' the ball so you know the other person will accept your offer."

Extension

- Introduce a second or even a third ball. Students will need to be even more attentive to making their tosses clear and direct.

Zip! Zap! Zop!

Improv Level: Beginner

Grade Level: All

Time Needed: 20 minutes

Materials: None

This is a fun, fast-paced activity that many actors use to build energy and sharpen focus before a performance. Students will learn to make clear, direct offers through the use of eye contact and by speaking clearly.

Directions

Everyone stands in a circle. The teacher begins by making eye contact with one student and claps her hands toward that student, saying "Zip!" This student then chooses another student and proceeds as the teacher did, this time saying, "Zap!" The next student says "Zop!," followed by "Zip!," and so on, with the three words repeating, always in order. A student may choose anyone to zip! (or zap! or zop!), and they must say the words in the correct sequence. Once students have learned the rules, it should proceed on a regular beat. If a student drops the beat or says the wrong word, the teacher should encourage the ensemble to start again from "Zip!"

Hint

- When students are excited about the game, it may be difficult to get them to focus after a student is declared out. Try indicating that the game is about to restart by patting your lap and saying "Reaaadddy" and then starting, letting the students know they need to focus or risk being caught not paying attention.

Side Coaching

- "Keep it moving. Don't think."

Extensions

- Once students have a feel for the game, introduce "boing!" At this point, student may proceed as above or they may "reject" a zip!, zap!, or zop! by saying "boing!" If they do this, the student attempting to pass the zip!, zap!, or zop! must try again, passing the same word to another player. Students may continue to boing! indefinitely.
- Have students use other one-syllable short-vowel words in order to practice hearing and saying various sounds, for example, "pit, pat, pot."

Woosh!

Improv Level: Beginner

Grade Level: 1st grade and up

Time Needed: 15–20 minutes

Materials: None

This game was originally introduced to us by a clown—not a class clown, but an actual clown! Improvisers use "Woosh!" as a warmup game because it physically and mentally loosens them up and helps the ensemble tune into each other. "Woosh!" has many parts to it, and while it is easy to learn, it appears complex (which students love). There are lots of opportunities in this game for students to create expressive performances, and as new elements are introduced, they can make a number of choices that impact the entire ensemble.

Directions:

This game involves several elements that are best introduced one at a time. The first is "Woosh!" Everyone stands in a circle. A "Woosh!" is passed around the circle as though it were a giant ball of energy. The teacher begins by passing a "Woosh!" to the left by turning and passing the mass of energy with her entire body by sweeping her arms in the direction of the child next to her. Not only does a "Woosh!" take a lot of energy to pass, but those receiving this imaginary ball of energy must brace themselves so it does not knock them over (figuratively). The energy is passed around the circle until it is returned to the teacher. A "Woosh!" can be passed either to the left or the right.

Next, introduce "Woah!" With "Woah!," students can now reject a "Woosh!" by placing both hands in front of their chest, facing out, and saying "Woah!" as though saying "No way!" Have students practice their most expressive "Woah!" a few times and then send a "Woosh!" around the circle, again encouraging students to either pass the "Woosh!" on or use a "Woah!" to reject it. If a "Woosh!" is rejected, the passer of the "Woosh!" must turn and send it in the opposite direction.

After a few minutes of "Woosh!" and "Woah!" introduce a third element, "Zap!" This is a way for the energy to be passed across the circle. This is done by making eye contact, clapping, pointing across the circle, and saying "Zap!"

Practice with these elements for a while. Remind students that they can:

- Woosh to the left.
- Woosh to the right.
- Woah a Woosh.
- Not Woah a Zap.
- Only Zap across the circle (not to a neighbor).

After students get used to these elements, introduce the final two elements: "Boing!" and "Groovalicious!" The person with the energy can call "Boing!" or "Groovalicious!" instead of passing it on. With "Boing!"

the student places her hands together above her head, shakes her hips and says, "Boing!" When this is done, everyone imitates the gesture until the student who initiated the "Boing!" suddenly passes on a "Woosh!" or a "Zap!"

When the person with the energy calls "Groovalicious!" everyone begins dancing in place to imaginary music of each person's choosing, calling out "Groovalicious!" They do this until the person with the energy passes it on with a "Woosh!" or a "Zap!"

Hint

- This game is not really as complicated as it sounds. Consider introducing it over a few days, introducing a new element each time.

Side Coaching

- "Imagine that the energy is very hot and is burning up. Pass it on as quickly as you can."

Extensions

- Invite the students to make up their own sounds and gestures.
- After the class becomes skilled at this game, have them try it with just the gestures, without the sounds.

Pass the Pulse

Improv Level: Beginner

Grade Level: All

Time Needed: 10–15 minutes (less once everyone knows the game)

Materials: None

"Pass the Pulse" is a quiet game that requires a great deal of concentration. Students enjoy the feeling of anticipation as they wait for the pulse to get to them and the whole group eagerly watches for the moment when the pulse completes its trip around the circle. It is a good way to introduce the concept of an ensemble because the activity only succeeds if everyone does his or her part. Because the game requires participants to slow down, it is also a good way to end an improvisation session.

Directions

The class sits or stands in a circle holding hands. The teacher passes a pulse of energy in one direction by gently squeezing the hand of a student next to her. That student then passes on the pulse by squeezing her neighbor's hand, and this continues around the circle until the pulse arrives back at the teacher.

Hints

- If students persist in losing the pulse, try passing the pulse with a sound, such as "beep," so the whole class can follow it.
- Consider demonstrating an appropriate squeeze to discourage students who may be prone to squeezing too hard.

Side Coaching

- "Feel the pulse move up your arms and through your body."
- "What happens to the pulse if someone stops holding hands?"

Extensions

- Try adding a second pulse in the same or opposite direction.
- Try adding a sound going in the opposite direction—at some point the pulse and the sound cross each other, so it requires even more concentration.
- When studying electricity, use this exercise to create a circuit. Introduce a battery, a switch, and even a lightbulb.

Synchronized Clapping

Improv Level: Beginner

Grade Level: All

Time Needed: 10–15 minutes

Materials: None

Learning to complete an action in unison is an important skill in working with others. In this activity, students must maintain careful focus and make eye contact so as not to "drop" the clap. Student will quickly learn that the game breaks down if anyone takes his or her eyes off the group.

Directions

Everyone stands in a circle. The teacher begins by turning to the right, facing and making eye contact with the student next to her, and "passing" a clap. This is done by both the teacher and the student clapping at exactly the same time. The first student then turns and passes the clap on to the next student in the same manner. The clap moves around the circle, at first slowly, and then more quickly as students improve. Eventually, students should be able to move at a consistent pace and be able to keep a beat as a class.

Hints

- Have everyone move very slowly and deliberately at first.
- The key to this activity is the eye contact.

Side Coaching

- "Don't forget to look at each other."
- "Keep the rhythm going."

Extensions

- Allow students to send the clap back in the opposite direction by clapping a second time with the person who passed them the clap.
- Introduce an additional clap in the same or opposite direction.
- Give one student a stopwatch. Have him time how quickly the clap moves around the circle once, and then divide into beats per minute. The class can chart its progress over time.
- Clap a short rhythm for students to replicate as a group. To do this, they will need to change the rate of their "passing" to match the rhythm they are trying to copy.

Mirrors

Improv Level: Beginner

Grade Level: 1st grade and up

Time Needed: 15 minutes

Materials: Small bell

This is a traditional theater exercise that is remarkably effective at helping students connect to one another. While it is mostly nonverbal, this activity actually teaches students to listen to one another. In order to work collaboratively, performers need to be able to tune into and coordinate their actions with a partner. This activity can be understood in terms of learning to say yes to all offers. Learning to function as an ensemble, to "think with one mind" or to "speak with one voice," is essential in improvisation.

Directions

Students are divided into pairs. The students decide who is A and who is B. Facing each other, about 2 feet apart, and making eye contact, the student who is A begins by very slowly making a series of movements with her body that Student B matches as carefully as possible, as though he were looking in a mirror. When the teacher rings the bell, the lead changes, with the B's immediately taking the lead and continuing to slowly move their bodies as the A's follow. Students should be instructed that their movements should be so slow that an observer should not be able to tell who is leading whom. As the activity continues, the teacher should ring the bell more frequently until the students are switching every few seconds. Once the activity has gone on for several minutes, with the lead changing by ringing the bell, students can be instructed to try to proceed without either student leading.

Hints

- Introduce the activity first as a whole group, with the class facing the teacher or another leader and mirroring the actions of that one person.
- Encourage students to change physical levels (e.g., bend down or stand on toes).
- Experiment with the timing of switching leaders. Often starting this switch slowly and building to a more rapid movement, perhaps every 8 to 10 seconds, helps the transition to working without a leader.

Side Coaching

- "Keep eye contact."
- "I shouldn't be able to tell who is leading. Leaders, make sure you help the followers keep up."

Extension

- Try the game as a vocal activity. Students pair up facing each other as before. One is designated as the leader and begins, very slowly, to tell a story, while the follower says the same words as the leader at exactly the same time. The leaders switch until finally the activity can be done without a leader.

Maah

Improv Level: Beginner

Grade Level: All

Time Needed: 5–10 minutes

Materials: None

There is something exhilarating in creating a sound in unison with other people—think of a choir or a group meditation chant. "Maah" is a vocal activity that challenges students to improve their listening skills as they attempt to speak with one voice. "Maah" helps students see the difference between performing as a collection of individuals and performing as an ensemble, where individual contributions are significant because they support the group.

Directions

Everyone sits in a tight circle. The teacher chants the word "maah," stretching it out to make one long sound as students repeat it. Together, the class attempts to create one continuous sound, even while individuals have to drop out and reenter to take a breath.

This continues as the teacher or a student chosen as the leader introduces hand motions to alter the sound. These hand motions, which can be determined ahead of time, correspond with various changes in the volume, pitch, and rhythm of the sound. For example, raising or lowering one's arms can raise or lower the volume.

Hint

- If the class has difficulty making a sound in unison, consider asking a few students to demonstrate first.

Side Coaching

- "Listen carefully. Try to make your sound match the sound of the group."

Extensions

- Have students choose new words for the class to chant and invent different signals to change its presentation.
- Use this activity to introduce various elements of musical vocabulary and give students an opportunity to be a conductor of their class.

Counting, How High?

Improv Level: Intermediate

Grade Level: 2nd grade and up

Time Needed: 10–15 minutes

Materials: None

This is a challenging activity that requires no previous improv experience and can help bring an ensemble into existence. The class can be successful only if they listen carefully, work together, and recover quickly from failure. Don't be discouraged if this activity is not a quick success; introduce and reintroduce it several times. Even though the game is difficult, most groups want to keep going until they succeed.

Directions

Students sit or stand in a tight circle. They are told that they are going to try to count to 10 together. The teacher explains that someone will start by saying "one," and then anyone can call out the next consecutive number until they reach 10. The catch is that if two people speak at once, the group must return to 1 and begin again.

Hints

- Have students sit with their backs to one another or close their eyes to avoid distractions and discourage blaming.
- Introduce the activity first to a smaller grouping of students and then have them teach the game to the entire class by demonstrating it for them.

Side Coaching

- "Try to listen to the group."
- "Don't try too hard to be the one to say a number. Try to help the group succeed."

Extensions

- Try using the alphabet or the Spanish alphabet, having students begin with the letter "a" and see how far into the alphabet they can get.
- Try this activity with multiples or prime numbers.
- Keep a chart that shows how high the group goes over a number of weeks so they can keep track of their progress.

My Song, Our Song

<table>
<tr><td>

Improv Level: Beginner

Grade Level: All

Time Needed: 15 minutes

Materials: None

</td><td>

Everyone starts off singing their own song, but gradually the group comes together to sing one song. This game moves from controlled chaos to a smooth, unison performance. Students will be amazed at how well this game works.

</td></tr>
</table>

Directions

Students are instructed to each think in their head of a familiar song that they think everyone will recognize. Everyone begins moving slowly around the room, with each one singing and repeating their song (it is likely that everyone will be singing a different song). Students are told that as they move around the room, if they recognize a song they hear, they are to stop singing their song and join in with the person whose song they recognize. This continues until everyone is singing the same song.

Side Coaching

- "Listen carefully. As soon as you recognize another song, you have to start singing it.
- "Accept all offers as quickly as possible."

Group Freeze

Improv Level: Beginner

Grade Level: All

Time Needed: 10 minutes

Materials: None

"Group Freeze" is a physical activity where all students get the chance to lead and follow. To make the game work, everyone must literally keep their eyes on the group and be willing to accept an offer as soon as it's made.

Directions

The class spreads out and begins walking around the room. At any moment, one student may stop walking. As soon as anyone stops, everyone is to stop immediately. The game continues when that player begins walking again, initiating everyone else to commence walking. The group continues to walk until another person stops and everyone freezes again.

Side Coaching

- "Keep your eyes on the group."

Extension

- Try this activity singing a song or clapping in a circle instead of walking. When singing, for example, everyone sings a familiar song until one student stops. When they do, the group must stop until that person is ready to start singing again.

Yes, Let's

Improv Level: Beginner

Grade Level: All

Time Needed: 10 minutes

Materials: None

Students' imaginations will run wild as they have the opportunity to lead their classmates on an adventure through their own classroom. This activity is a fun way for students to practice accepting offers as a group. Students can also develop their skills at leading and following.

Directions

Students begin by walking about the room in a random pattern. At any point, anyone can call out an instruction, for example, "Let's all swim like fish," and everyone must respond, "Yes, let's!" and then move around the room pretending to swim like fish until someone calls out a new idea. The game continues with lots of suggestions. Often it will end after much movement and silliness when someone gets the bright idea to say, "Let's all lie down and go to sleep!"

Hint

- If it gets too chaotic, you can call out something calmer like, "Let's all go fishing."

Side Coaching

- "What are some things no one has thought of yet?"

Extensions

- Instead of physical activities, have students call out emotional states: "Let's all be sad."
- If you are studying a particular period in history, you can have students call out activities from that period: "Let's all cross the Delaware."
- For younger children, occupations or animals they're studying may be incorporated into the game, with suggestions such as, "Let's all be firefighters."

What Are You Doing?

Improv Level: Beginner

Grade Level: 2nd grade and up

Time Needed: 15 minutes

Materials: None

This is a zany activity that involves a mismatch between words and actions. The activity provides an opportunity for students to take turns leading and following. It is also a structured activity that is an excellent introduction to more complicated free-form scene work. Students will enjoy inventing ideas for their classmates to act out and may be surprised at the creative scenes they invent.

Directions

Everyone sits in a circle. One student goes first and stands in the middle, silently miming an activity, such as juggling. Another student is chosen from the circle and approaches her and asks, "What are you doing?" The first student then says something she is *not* doing, such as walking a dog. The second student then begins miming the activity the first student *said* she was doing. The first student exits and a third student approaches, asking, "What are you doing?" as before. Each time the student says something he or she *isn't* doing, which the next student must then do.

Hint

- Encourage students not to think of an answer to the question "What are you doing?" until asked. They may be surprised at what they invent without forethought.

Side Coaching

- "Tell her you're doing the silliest activity you can think of."

Extension

- Once students are comfortable with the activity, have all the participants remain in the middle after a new activity is started, so that each time more and more students are in the middle miming a new activity together, until eventually the entire class is miming together.

Group Sculpture

Improv Level: Intermediate

Grade Level: 3rd grade and up

Time Needed: 25 minutes

Materials: Stopwatch

This activity is a sort of silent, three-dimensional "Yes, and" where students have the chance to mold a giant, life-sized hunk of clay into a living, breathing class sculpture. As they sculpt their masterpiece, students will learn not to force their own idea but to add to the ideas of their class-mates, saying "Yes, and," not with words but with their hands. Students will be amazed at the beautiful "offer" they collectively create.

Directions

The class is divided into two groups. One group forms a circle fac-ing out, and the other group forms a circle around them facing in. The students on the outside are the Sculptors and the students on the inside are the Clay. The teacher times the action, with the students on the outside having 30 seconds to sculpt the person directly in front of them. When 30 seconds have passed, the students on the outside stop sculpting and move clockwise around the circle, examining the sculpture in the middle. They go all the way around the circle, past the last person they sculpted, and stop at the next person.

Again they have 30 seconds to sculpt the student in front of them. This time, however, they are given the direction to make their portion of the sculpture fit with the rest of the sculpture. This continues with students sculpting and observing until the students in the outer circle arrive back at their original spots. They then step back and observe what they have created together.

Hint

- Encourage students to only make small adjustments to the sculpture.

Side Coaching

- "What offers do you notice? How can you add to what your group has sculpted so far?"

Extension

- Have students sculpt a famous historical scene, such as the signing of the Declaration of Independence.

Make a Machine

Improv Level: Beginner

Grade Level: All

Time Needed: 10–15 minutes

Materials: None

This game challenges participants to use their entire bodies and voices in a collaborative activity. It is a wonderful example of how a group can create something collectively that is not just the sum total of each individual's contribution. Because the whole class works together and can be slowed down collectively, this is another good exercise for concluding a session of improv activities.

Directions

The class stands in a circle. The teacher tells the students that they are going to make a human machine. Anyone can go first and everyone will join in, one at a time, when they are inspired. The machine begins when one person enters the center of the circle and begins with a machinelike noise and movement, such as twisting one's torso and making a repetitive beeping noise. Another student joins in by entering the circle, physically connecting to that student's movement, and making an additional noises and movements that are consistent with the rhythm and tone of the first. The students do not need to be touching but should be close, as though representing parts of one machine. The game proceeds until the entire class has joined in. At this point, the teacher may encourage the machine to move gradually faster or slower, louder or softer.

Hint

- It is best to end this game with a slow, quiet machine, by having the students become gradually quieter until the machine moves to a halt. This can provide a nice transition into quieter activities.

Side Coaching

- "Listen and watch the machine. What sound or movement can you contribute?"
- "Change levels. Have your part of the machine be tall or short."

Extensions

- Challenge students to create an angry machine, a happy machine, a math machine, etc.
- Have one student serve as a salesperson for the machine: He or she names the machine and says what it is used for, how it works, where it can be bought, and how much it costs.
- Use this exercise as an introduction to a study of the Industrial Revolution.

Still Life

Improv Level: Intermediate

Grade Level: 2nd grade and up

Time Needed: 15 minutes

Materials: None

In this activity, students work together silently in small groups to turn into a painting. In order to be successful, everyone in the ensemble will need to quickly accept all offers. If students ignore or negate one another, they will not be able to complete the picture in the allotted time. The struggle to create a scene without talking pushes students to explore nonverbal communication.

Directions

Three or more students stand in the front of the room and face the class. The students solicit a word from the audience, such as "cow," and then, without talking, must create a sculpture that represents that word.

Hint

- Consider giving a time limit of, perhaps, 30 seconds for each still life.

Side Coaching

- "Look out for offers and accept them quickly."

Extension

- Once students have confidence with the exercise, encourage them to make suggestions other than concrete nouns, such as "beauty" or "anger."

Remote Control

Improv Level: Intermediate

Grade Level: 2nd grade and up

Time Needed: 10 minutes

Materials: None

There's no doubt that kids love watching TV. With "Remote Control," they have the chance to create their own show from the small screen right in their own classroom. The challenge is that they have to listen carefully to the group to raise and lower their collective volume. This teaches students to see and hear the whole group.

Directions

The class selects a location for an event they are all attending that involves making a lot of noise, such as being in the stands at a basketball game or at a beach party. One student is designated to be the TV watcher, who is to pretend that she is watching the action on her television screen at home. She uses her imaginary remote control to turn on the TV by snapping her fingers and saying, "On." The rest of the class begins performing their scene. When the action begins, the TV watcher may raise or lower the volume using the imaginary remote control. This is done by raising her hands high above her head for a higher volume, or bringing them low to the ground for a lower volume. She may also "mute" the action by clapping her hands and saying, "Mute." The action ends when the TV watcher turns of the TV by snapping her fingers and saying, "Off."

Hint

- Remind students in the scene to continue the action even when the volume is low or muted.

Side Coaching

- "Keep your eye on the remote and listen to the group."

Extension

- Add functions to the remote control such as freeze, fast forward, and rewind. Have students invent movements for these new remote control features.

Activities on Emotions

These activities all provide opportunities for children to explore and play with emotions. Activities like "Pass the Face" and "Gestures" prompt students to tune into how they and their classmates express themselves, while activities like "Emotional Journey" and "Emotional Mélange" provide a space for students to create new emotional performances. As you create with one another's emotionality, your class will develop a lexicon of emotional performances that can become a part of your class's culture.

Shout It Out

Improv Level: Beginner

Grade Level: All

Time Needed: 10 minutes

Materials: None

A single word can express so much: fear, love, rage. By experimenting with tone, volume, and affect, and by exploring various ways to add emotion and expression to words, students will discover the powerful role of the nonverbal and verbal aspects of language.

Directions

The class stands in a circle. The teacher selects a common word, such as "yes," "no," or "stop." After the word is announced to the class, any student may step forward and say the word however she chooses, be it loud, angry, silly, and so on. Once he steps back into the circle, the rest of the class steps forward and repeats the word in precisely the same way it was delivered. After five or six presentations by different students of the original word in different emotions, pick a new word.

Hint

- Resist the temptation to reject offers that may seem inappropriate.

Side Coaching

- "Think of all the different ways you use or hear that word."
- "Show us the emotion in your presentation. You can say a lot with that one little word."

Extension

- Try this exercise with short phrases, or lines from a novel or play. See what your students can discover about a character or a story when experimenting with different ways of delivering the same line.

Gestures

Improv Level: Beginner

Grade Level: All

Time Needed: 10 minutes

Materials: None

Similar in structure to "Shout It Out," this activity whittles communication down to a simple, silent gesture. Students can discover the power of these simple movements in communicating personality and emotion. As they do so, they will also develop their familiarity with a variety of adjectives.

Directions

The class stands in a circle. The teacher asks for volunteers to step forward to make a brief gesture that represents an emotion. These can include:

- sadness
- competition
- exhaustion
- affection
- ambition
- greed
- love

After the student steps forward, the class steps into the middle and repeats the gesture.

Hint

- Depending on the class, it may be helpful to make gestures that represent people in the class off-limits.

Side Coaching

- "What is the affectionate person doing? Show us with your whole body."

Extensions

- Suggest that students perform a gesture that represents someone they know.
- Ask students to give examples of gestures of various characters from a novel they are reading together as a class.

Emotions/Motions

Improv Level: Beginner

Grade Level: All

Time Needed: 20 minutes

Materials: None

Everyone has an image of sadness, happiness, anger, etc. But what would it look like to paint a fence or play soccer while giving expression to these feelings? This exercise provides an opportunity for children to explore different ways of showing emotions together. Younger children can also expand their vocabulary for feeling words.

Directions

Everyone stands in a circle. One student leaves the room for a few minutes. While she is gone, the rest of the class picks a common emotion, such as joy or fear. The student who left then returns to the room and chooses an activity for the class to do together, such as digging a ditch or playing tag. The class then mimes that activity while portraying their emotion. The observing student must then guess the emotion.

Hint

- If a child has difficulty guessing the emotion, have him choose a second or even a third activity for the class to do.

Side Coaching

- "Think ahead: What might an angry ditchdigger do or say?"

Extension

- Using a book that everyone in the class has read, have the students perform a scene from the book several times, each time portraying a different emotion. Don't worry about matching the emotion of the story to the emotion being acted out. This disconnect is what makes the game meaningful.

Pass the Face

Improv Level: Beginner

Grade Level: All

Time Needed: 15 minutes

Materials: None

The human face is wondrously expressive. From even the quickest glance we can discern a host of emotions and non-verbal communication. This exercise provides a workout for your students' faces. As they accept the offers, however silly or pained, they are collectively creating a new experience with these expressions.

Directions

Everyone stands in a circle. The leader begins by silently making a silly face and turning to her neighbor to the left, who carefully examines the face, taking as much time as necessary, and copies it as closely as possible. This second student then turns slowly to his left. As he turns, he gradually changes the face into a new expression. The third student then copies the face and passes a new one on. This continues until the face is passed around the entire circle.

Hint

- Review with the students the basics of giving and receiving offers. Remind them that the object of the exercise is not for them to make the silliest face, but to build with the face they are given.

Side Coaching

- "Don't try to change the face completely. Let the face you receive inspire what you pass on."

Extension

- Try the exercise again with the children using their entire bodies to make dynamic poses, including expressive facial gestures.

Emotional Journey

Improv Level: Intermediate

Grade Level: 2nd grade and up

Time Needed: 20–30 minutes

Materials: None

It's conventional wisdom in schools and elsewhere that you "just can't change how you feel." In this exercise, students are challenged to do just that.

Directions

Students are chosen to perform one at a time. They are given a character and two contrasting emotions, and asked to walk from one end of the room to the other while acting out a scene as that character. As they begin walking, they perform the first emotion, and then they gradually shift from the first emotion to the second as they walk across the room. By the time they have completed their walk, they have completely shifted to performing the second emotion.

Hint

- If students are having difficulty, have the class offer a task for the student to perform.

Side Coaching

- "Make your transition gradual."

Extension

- Have students perform as familiar characters. For example, perform as Bugs Bunny going on an emotional journey.

Emotional Coach

Improv Level: Advanced

Grade Level: 3rd grade and up

Time Needed: 25 minutes

Materials: None

We've all had students who seem to switch emotions every few moments: crying one second, playing and laughing the next. This exercise takes that experience to the extreme, giving students an opportunity to try out and respond to a range of (often) absurd emotions as they create scenes together.

Directions

Two students are selected to perform a scene. They are given a suggestion for their character and a location from the audience. Two other students are selected to perform as the Emotional Coaches. Each of these students creates a list of emotions based on suggestions from the audience. The Coaches stand off to the side while the two performers create the scene. At any moment, either Coach can call out an emotion from their list, and the performer they are coaching must switch to a performance that incorporates that emotion.

Hints

- Coaching works best if students are allowed to deliver a few lines before their emotion is switched.
- Remind the Coaches that their emotion does not need to match the action of the scene. Often an absurd pairing is most dramatic.

Side Coaching

- "Keep the scene moving."
- "Remember, respond to the offers your partner is making, *including the emotional offers.*"

Emotional Mélange

Improv Level: Intermediate

Grade Level: 1st grade and up

Time Needed: 20 minutes

Materials: Markers and chart paper

We relate to emotions as if they happen one at a time. But aren't we sometimes sad and excited at the same time? And some days, we just don't know how we feel; one moment we're elated and another jealous. This activity is a chance to perform two emotions at the same time. Who knows? Perhaps your students will invent some new emotions along the way.

Directions

The class brainstorms a list of emotions that are then written on chart paper in front of the classroom. Students perform one at a time and choose a simple character to perform, which they announce to the class. The teacher chooses two emotions from the list. The students then perform a 1-minute scene as their character, conveying both emotions at the same time.

Hint

- Remind students that they are making up their performances from scratch. They need not find the "correct" way of expressing anxious and joyful, for example.

Side Coaching

- "Make sure we can see *both* emotions in everything your character does."

Extension

- Once students have performed a few 1-minute scenes, have two characters present a scene, each one representing two different, mixed-up emotions (e.g., giddy and jealous).

Emotional Bus

Improv Level: Intermediate

Grade Level: 3rd grade and up

Time Needed: 25 minutes

Materials: None

Many students frequently do not have a sufficient vocabulary of feelings. This activity introduces a range of feeling words and allows students to play around with their meanings. The shared, collective experience of being depressed, ecstatic, or lackadaisical can bring depth to these complicated feelings.

Directions

Several students (at least five) stand in front of the class. Chairs are arranged to suggest seats on a bus, and one student is designated the Bus Driver and sits in the driver's seat. As the bus drives along its route, the Driver picks up each of the other performers, one at a time, as though picking each one up from a different bus stop. As they enter, each passenger is given an emotion by the audience to bring onto the bus. As each new student enters, everyone on the bus, including the Bus Driver, must act out that emotion together.

Hint

- Discuss with the students ahead of time some common discussions that might take place on a bus.

Side Coaching

- "Rather than saying, 'I am so *happy* today,' do something that shows you are happy."
- "Quiet down when a new person gets on the bus so you can hear what they are saying."

Extension

- Challenge the class to offer increasingly complicated feeling words. Keep an ongoing list of feeling words as students learn them that can be incorporated into the game.

Emotional Orchestra

Improv Level: Intermediate

Grade Level: 1st grade and up

Time Needed: 25 minutes

Materials: None

When most of us think of an orchestra, we picture a refined, serene grouping of skilled musicians. This activity uses emotional material to create an irreverent orchestra, where the music is created not by violins and timpani, but by your students' gripes, fears, and enthusiasm. This exercise allows students to fine-tune their emotional performances as they create expressive, passionate "music."

Directions

Several students stand in front of the class. One by one, each student chooses a unique emotion and decides on a sound he or she is going to make to represent that emotion (e.g., crying or shouting for joy). The teacher, who is performing as the Conductor, points to each student in the Orchestra, one at a time, to present his or her noise to the class as a brief "solo." The group then performs as an ensemble, performing their separate emotions together and carefully following the Conductor's directions. The Conductor can invent various movements to indicate when some students should get louder or quieter, faster or slower, or emote at a higher or lower pitch.

Hints

- After playing a few times, students may take turns conducting.
- Remind the students that playing together as an ensemble requires careful attention to the direction of a leader (in this case, the Conductor). Even though they are making unusual sounds, they are performing as musicians who should take pride in their collective sound.

Side Coaching

- "Watch me carefully. Take control of your instrument."

Extension

- Have each student choose what is bothering them to complain ("gripe") about. They can gripe about the weather, a pestering sibling, or something that's been troubling them in the classroom. When it's their turn, each person complains verbally about their topic. When conducting, stay with one person for a little while to give him or her a chance to create many different ways to gripe.

The Nuisance Game

Improv Level: Intermediate

Grade Level: 2nd grade and up

Time Needed: 25 minutes

Materials: None

It's never easy to get work done in a chaotic environment. It is especially trying when someone is intentionally working to distract you. This exercise turns that irritating experience into a game, where students can play with the performance of the nuisance. A less difficult version of this activity is done with the whole class and is included as an extension.

Directions

This game is performed as a two-person scene. Ask the class for a suggestion of a task or a job that requires a great deal of concentration (e.g., brain surgery or studying at the library). One student performs as the person attempting to do the task requiring concentration, and the other is the Nuisance. The job of the Nuisance is to try to distract the other person from their task while still participating in creating the scene. For example, the Nuisance might be chewing gum loudly while the other person is trying to read.

Hint

- Encourage students to incorporate distracting behaviors that are common problems in the class, such as sharpening pencils, asking superfluous questions, and so forth.

Side Coaching

- "Start out being a little bit of a bother and then get more and more annoying as the scene continues."
- "Remember that you're in the library (or operating room, or movie theater)."

Extension

- The class sits on the rug or at their desks as they would for a lesson, such as math. The teacher writes a complicated problem or a difficult task on the board and then asks the class to solve the problem. One or two students in the class are designated as the Nuisance (or the Pest, for younger students). That student or students' job is to distract the class, making it as difficult as possible for them to complete their work. The game continues until the class calls out, "We give up!"

Optimist/Pessimist

Improv Level: Intermediate

Grade Level: 2nd grade and up

Time Needed: 25 minutes

Materials: None

Even at a young age, students have begun to gain a reputation as optimists or pessimists (even if they don't use those words). This activity pokes playful fun at these all-too-familiar roles by allowing students to mold exaggerated performances into a sort of optimist/pessimist tug-of-war.

Directions

Two students are chosen to tell a story to the class. One is designated as the Optimist, the other as the Pessimist. The students tell a story together, using the "Yes, and" format, each one telling one line at a time. As they tell the story, the Optimist tells a line of something good that happens, then the Pessimist gives a line of something bad.

Hints

- Remind students to be wary of negating. Presenting an pessimistic outlook does not mean disagreeing with what's been said but rather adding to it in a way that is consistent with a particular point of view.
- Younger students will, of course, need to be taught what an optimist and pessimist are.

Side Coaching

- "Remember, don't negate. Accept what your partner has said and add to it, even while you have a different point of view."

Chapter 4

Improvising Language and Literacy

Although learning to read and write has always been the primary task of elementary school, in the past decade it's become a national obsession. Many teachers are required or choose to spend as much as two-thirds of their day on language arts activities. Teachers are also bombarded with information about the "right" way to teach children to read and write, with researchers and practitioners positioned across the spectrum, from whole language, to balanced literacy, to phonics instruction. We believe that teachers should have a range of techniques at their disposal, and our primary concern is helping teachers and students to create environments where the class can perform as readers and writers and listeners and speakers, whatever the technique. Improv can provide a useful tool for teachers and children in creating environments where language arts activities are playfully and creatively approached in a way that supports the class's development.

If you have read this far in the book, you realize that we see learning as a cultural activity. By *cultural* we mean that learning is something that human beings create, just as we create theater, dance, government, and a myriad of other activities. Learning occurs through the process of continuously creating environments where it can occur. However, learning to read and write can easily become overly associated with methods of teaching such as balanced literacy and phonics, or even with particular curricula such as Orton-Gillingham and the Letter People. When this happens, teachers can get so focused on applying a tool (curriculum) that will produce a particular outcome (learning to read or write) that they lose sight of the fact that every group of teachers and children has to produce the environment that can allow that tool to be useful to them. There are an infinite number of ways for people to come together to create successful literacy learning environments, and doing improv together is one of them. In this chapter we will lay out some ideas about this and provide you with activities that can get you started.

LANGUAGE LEARNING

In thinking about the literacy learning environment, it is helpful to look more closely at the enormously successful language learning/meaning-making environment of infancy and early childhood. This is not because we believe that learning to read and write can be done in the same way as learning to speak one's first language. We do not think that they can. But we believe that there is something valuable, from a methodological point of view, to be learned from how babies and their caregivers create environments where, within a few short years, and with no formal instruction, almost all children become fluent speakers of at least one language.

As we discussed in Chapter 1, the environment where babies learn to speak is a wonderful example of how human beings, in this case babies, are supported to be both who they are (nonspeakers) and who they are becoming (speakers). When a baby says, "Oooh, ga beee da," adults and older children might say, "Yes, that's a dog, do you want to pet the dog?" They do not wait for the baby to be ready to speak before they create conversations with her, and they do not expect her to participate in the conversation in the same way as an adult or older child. In this way, babies are invited and supported to perform as speakers well before they actually are, and in the course of this, they become speakers. One of the most important characteristics of this activity is that an ensemble—the baby, siblings, friends, parents, even strangers on the street—create it together. Together everyone supports the baby to do what she does not yet know how to do.

Another hallmark of the language learning environment is that it is playful. Being a becoming speaker is joyful, often silly, and not at all about getting it right. Listen to a 9-month-old and her mother or a group of preschoolers talking together, and the experience is that it is fun to feel, play, and experiment with words and meanings. It is also playful in the sense that it is noninstrumental; while conversing with infants and toddlers clearly helps them develop as speakers, we adults do not talk with them in order to teach them to speak. We do it because conversing is one activity that human beings do, and right from the start babies are included in the community of speakers.

PERFORMING AS READERS AND WRITERS

What does all of this have to do with learning to read and write? The methodology of creating environments where children can be both who they are and who they are becoming is critical to all kinds of learning. In the case of literacy, children need to be a part of creating environments where they can perform as readers and writers. There is research that demonstrates that this is what happens in the homes and communities of many, mostly middle-class children. Children are invited into the community of readers and writers through the activity of participating in literacy activities, just like they participated in speaking activities as infants and toddlers.

In school, children are rarely "invited in" in that way, that is, given opportunities to perform ahead of where they are. Schools, with their focus on skill-based learning, work to identify what a child can and

cannot do, or does and does not know. The job of the teacher is to provide instruction that is appropriate to this level and that will remediate
any perceived deficits. In this way children are not related to as who
they are becoming, but rather as *only* who they are. While we are not
arguing against the need for assessments or targeted instruction, when
this focus becomes all of what is happening in the classroom, children
are often deprived of the joy of performing as readers and writers.

This joy is a component of what is sometimes referred to as pre-
literacy and brings up one of our concerns with the literacy learning
environments of many classrooms. Reading and writing are not generally seen in the context of their rich developmental history, that is, as a
lifelong process by which human beings develop as symbol-makers and
users. Children's use of the formal symbols of a particular language is
not the beginning of literacy learning. Learning to make and use symbols
happens when a toddler picks up a shoe, holds it to her ear, and says,
"Hi, Mommy"; when a 3-year-old "reads" her favorite book to her baby
brother; and when two 4-year-olds write down food orders in their pretend restaurant. Yet if teachers relate to the literacy activities of school
as if they are isolated activities separate from these creative and playful
endeavors, they end up ignoring this history and have many fewer tools
at their disposal for supporting further literacy development.

Improv gives children opportunities to be both who they are and who
they are becoming. In the case of reading and writing, improv does not
require a particular skill level as a prerequisite for participation. Instead,
many of the activities in this chapter enable children to perform as accomplished readers and writers long before they actually are. For example, a
child who is struggling with learning to decode two-syllable words can
still perform as a poet in "Gibberish Poem." And a child who has trouble
finding the main point of a story can create questions for her classmates
in one of the extensions of "Yes, and." It is obviously important to learn to
decode and to comprehend what you have read—*and* removing this goal,
even for a brief exercise, allows for the possibility of learning how to read
by reading. There are also ways that readers and writers perform where
to sit, how to sit, and what voice to use, etc. In an activity such as "Fake
It," children create scenes where everyone, no matter their reading level,
can perform as readers and writers.

READING AND WRITING AS ENSEMBLE ACTIVITIES

Improv also develops the ensemble environment in the often solitary
activity of learning to read. Learning to read and write is usually seen as
an individuated activity. While children may work in reading groups or
in paired reading activities, for the most part reading is not related to as
something a group of people is creating together. In addition, classrooms
are increasingly linguistically diverse with regard to reading and writing ability, English language learners, and students with language-based
disabilities. Teachers tend to divide children into homogeneous groups

for language instruction, and while this might make sense for teaching phonics or reading appropriately leveled stories, it also creates divisions that limit the resources available to teachers and students.

Improv allows opportunities for students to work together (including as a whole class) that are not determined by their reading or writing ability. Improv provides a way for everyone to play with language, to create and read together. We are not arguing that heterogeneous groups are automatically successful learning environments. Many mixed-ability groupings fail to support either the more or the less skilled children, not to mention those who are quiet or never stop talking. Improv, however, is structured in such a way that participants are supported to contribute from where they are, but in a way that supports the group. For example, in "Blah, Blah, Blah," a non–English speaker might be the star; in a collective storytelling activity, anyone can contribute. In this way, improv helps to create a Zone of Proximal Development where the class creates an environment where everyone can develop as readers and writers. In this environment, everyone's job is to contribute what they can for the good of the group.

In addition, improv activities provide the class with an opportunity to work directly with the teacher in a playful, creative manner. In many classrooms teachers either conduct literacy instruction to the whole class at a level meant to meet the needs of the middle of the group, or they work with one leveled reading group while the rest of the class completes independent activities. During improv activities, children are practicing reading and writing with the support of an adult and other children. Through such playful encounters, teachers can learn more about what their students are capable of, and children can get valuable feedback that is aimed at improving the group's performance, not correcting the individual child.

One of the stated reasons that reading groups are divided homogeneously is so that no one is either held back by their less skilled peers or lost and confused by work that is beyond their reading level. These issues are transformed when children are asked to give their most developed performances for the good of the group. Similar to a star basketball player who has to get more accurate at making layups as his team gets better at setting him up for a shot, a brilliant storyteller has to develop a more creative vocabulary as her class gets better at telling "Yes, and" stories.

The heterogeneous nature of the improv ensemble has the added benefit of preventing children from being labeled as more or less smart based on how well they currently read. In most classrooms being a poor reader immediately categorizes someone as less smart even though reading is only one part of ability. Improv provides opportunities for children to participate in language activities that are more advanced, but are not based purely on reading ability. The language activities that children who are less skilled at reading participate in are often less rich and less creative—they involve simple books or worksheets that may be appropriate for the child's reading level, but are too simplistic to be of interest to them. An activity such as "Hot Seat" is sophisticated and does not require a particular reading level. Improv provides a way for the whole class to participate in rich and creative language games together.

READING, WRITING, SPEAKING, AND LISTENING RELATIONALLY

Recently there has been a growing recognition that language arts instruction, while primarily focused on reading and writing, also needs to include listening and speaking. Teachers are being asked to teach, and children are being assessed on, a range of skills that are identified as listening and speaking skills. Helping children develop in these areas is not easy. We are not alone in pointing out that as a society, Americans are not very good at listening, and that our speaking skills are idiosyncratic at best. For many people, listening is the activity of waiting for one's turn to speak. Even those people who engage in what is called "active listening" are often focused on finding ways to ensure that the person they are speaking with feels listened to by nodding in the right places, echoing back what is said, or saying, "Uh-huh." Similarly, speaking is often understood as expressing what is already in one's head. In all of these cases, neither listening nor speaking is about creating something with the person with whom one is conversing.

Given the focus in improv on creating and building with the ensemble, listening and speaking are not separate activities. In order to create an improv scene, one must listen for offers and speak in order to build on those offers. Improvisers have a passion for listening; without listening there is nothing to build with, no material to create the scene. Some improv exercises, such as "Hot Seat" and "Boppity, Bop, Bop," have as their primary focus developing people's skills at listening, but almost all of the games in this chapter involve speaking and listening as relational activities that allow students to create scenes and stories together.

Reading and writing, just like speaking and listening, are relational activities. Reading and writing are conversations between an author or authors (and perhaps an illustrator) and the person reading. However, because reading and writing are often done alone, we tend to forget that they are social. Improv can make the social nature of reading and writing more overt. It is possible not just to bring to life the content of a text but to add dimension to the activity of reading, separate from and independent of its meaning. For example, students can improvise a conversation with the author of a recently read book in "The Author Comes to Life" or collectively create a story in "'Yes, and' Extension."

CREATING LANGUAGE

We are paradoxically both a *language-creating* species and a *language-using* species. Vygotsky teaches that language is a tool that human beings have created and continue to create. We use that tool very effectively when we fill out an application for a driver's license, and we use it when we read the questions on the SAT. However, if we start relating to ourselves only as language users, there is a loss. A primary task of school is to teach children to be appropriate language users, but too often the way this is done winds up suppressing children's language-creating ability. The current attention to literacy activities that are primarily focused on specific learning outcomes and the assessment of particular skills means that in far too many classrooms, language has ceased to be something children are joyfully creating and has become only something they are memorizing or using in the "right" way. They lose that visceral connection to language that they (and all of us) had as beginning speakers, or, at best, they continue to have it with friends on the playground, but not in the classroom.

Improv activities are about creating with language. In some activities children actually create languages or words using gibberish or speaking in a made-up foreign language that no one is actually conversant in. In others, such as "I'm Sorry, Did You Say . . . ?" or "Gibberish Poem," children make meaning by creating stories or poems collectively. These activities bring some of the playfulness of the meaning-making/language-learning environment of early childhood into the classroom. Improv also provides opportunities to make meaning out of already existing text. For example, in "Live Action Illustration," the class can improvise pictures to go along with a favorite chapter book, and in "Book Extending 'Yes, and'" in the "'Yes, and' Extension" activity, they extend the story of their favorite characters.

In addition, improv provides an opportunity to play with the rules of language that have been created over time and that provide the key to decoding and making sense of symbols on a page. In activities such as "Alliteration" and "Collective Spelling," children play with letter–sound connections, phonemic awareness, and spelling rules. In this way children can learn the phonics game without it becoming a chore, boring, or a test. Improv (and not just the games in this chapter) provides opportunities to make the rules of language (including nonverbal language) explicit. Children can play with the rules and create new ones. Whatever the skill being learned, children are using written or spoken language to create something with other people. This experience can shift children's relationships to one another and to the words on the page.

IMPROVISING LITERACY ALL THE TIME

Having worked in schools, we know that many teachers are thinking, "I don't have time for improv games; my language arts block is already too full." We urge you to think of this not as separate from your literacy time but as a way to make your literacy time more effective and efficient, and as a way of making other times (transitions, community-building time, even recess) more enriched with language and literacy activities.

Finally, while most of this chapter is focused on improv activities that you can use with students to give them an opportunity to perform as readers and writers, we also believe that literacy instruction would benefit if teachers developed their ability to improvise in a broader sense of the word. Teachers are often presented with new curricula, teaching methods, and mandates about what is the best way to teach children to read. Sometimes the quantity of recommendations can be overwhelming or the advice can seem contradictory. While we do not subscribe to one particular technique for teaching children to read and write, we do believe that there can be an improvisational response to what teachers are being asked to do. From this vantage point the new mandates and curricula become the material for the ongoing creation of an improvised literacy performance with the class. Teachers learn to relate to all of what they are being told about balanced literacy, decoding, best practices, and evidence-based education as offers.

Many of you probably already do this by mixing and matching different approaches, depending on what works with particular students. We are inviting you to take that further: In addition to using multiple curricular approaches, we believe it is possible to reorganize the structure of how learning occurs by including students in the improvised play of learning to read. For example, this might mean developing an improv scene in your class where a group of students who already know how to read has to learn how to perform as experts in phonics and teach the less skilled readers how to pronounce the letters of the alphabet. This is just one possible performance and might raise difficult issues for you and your students, but we are suggesting that improv can allow for the continuous reorganization of what is available in the classroom in new and creative ways.

"Yes, and" Collective Story and Other "Yes, and" Extensions

Improv Level: Beginner

Grade Level: All

Time Needed: 30–40 minutes

Materials: None

As we discussed in Chapter 2, "Yes, and" is the essential ingredient for building improvisation (and classroom) scenes. We have included the directions for the original "Yes, and" here, followed by a number of extensions you may want to try out. As you read and play them, we hope that you and your students will be inspired to create countless variations using the "Yes, and" theme, both in language arts and throughout the curriculum.

Directions

The class sits in a circle. The teacher explains that they are going to tell a story together. Each person will contribute one sentence and everyone (except the first person) will start their sentence with the words "Yes, and." The story should be told in the third person (avoid *I, me, we, us*), and the characters should be given names. The teacher solicits suggestions for a title from the class. The teacher then repeats the title and begins the story by saying the first sentence. The person to the teacher's right continues the story, starting his or her sentence with the words "Yes, and" and adding a sentence. The story proceeds with each consecutive person adding one sentence beginning with "Yes, and" to the story. Students should be encouraged not to try to move the story along too quickly or to steer it in their own direction, but instead to build gradually on what has been said. A successful story might not "go" very far but might still be very satisfying. The story ends whenever the teacher, or anyone in the class, feels it has reached a conclusion, or time has run out.

Hints

- The first few times you do this activity the teacher should definitely say the first line. Model a good first line by making sure to include who the story is about, where it takes place, and a little bit of action. For example, "Johnny woke up, looked out his window, and began to cry."
- Avoid using the names of people in the room.
- This activity can be very challenging for students who want to shape the story or make a bold or silly offer. Consider stopping students when they do this and reminding them to attend to what was said previously.

Side Coaching

- "How might you *use the offer* you just got from [name of person who just spoke before]?"

- "Add a line that *could not* have been said without the line before it."
- "What's the *very next* thing that happened in the story?"
- "Let the group tell the story."

Extensions

- *Full Body "Yes, and."* Have each student create and hold a pose that represents his or her addition to the story. Each student holds his or her pose until every student has had a chance to add a line.
- *"Yes, and" Song.* Create a "Yes, and" collective song where each student improvises a new line for the song.
- *Nonfiction "Yes, and."* The class tells a nonfiction story about something that the whole class experienced together.
- *Three-Word (or One-Word) "Yes, and."* Each person says only three words or one word (depending on the variation you're playing). Little words like "I," "the," and "an" count. Remind students to end sentences by the inflection in their voice. While no one says, "Yes, and," it is implied.
- *Written "Yes, and."* The teacher starts a story and leaves it on a clipboard in front of the room. Students can add to it as they wish, as long as they don't negate what other students have said. The teacher can make inputs as often as necessary to add structure to the story.
- *Scribble Babble.* Students write stories as they would for a writers workshop–type activity, only in place of writing they draw scribbles. Each student then passes his or her story to a classmate, who "reads" it and then prepares to comment. Students then come together at the rug and discuss what they liked about the stories they read.
- *Tag Team "Yes, and."* Before playing, students are broken up into three groups, each with a separate assignment, that of deciding either who the characters are, where the story takes place, or what happens in the story. Each group completes their task by using "Yes, and." The groups then report back to the class and sit dispersed around the circle. The teacher writes each dramatic element on the board. The class then tells a "Yes, and" story using the elements created by each group.
- *Road Sign Stories.* The three variations below begin with the class seated in a circle. As with "Yes, and," the teacher solicits a topic or title from the class and delivers the first line. The teacher then holds up a road sign that provides direction to the next student on how to deliver his or her line. (As you try a few of the variations of this game, your class may invent other sentence starters or rules for the road signs. For example, they could display other conjunctions or key words that indicate directions for how the plot should move forward.) For materials, you will need cardboard or poster board for making signs. Depending on the variation being played, the two-sided signs say the following:

— *Fortunately/Unfortunately.* With this version, each line of the story begins with the word "fortunately" or "unfortunately," depending on which side of the sign the teacher displays to each student. Students must add a line to the story that is consistent with the meaning of those two words.

— *Color/Advance.* Here students are free to begin their line of the story with whatever word they choose. However, depending on which side of the sign the teacher displays to them, they must either "color" or "advance" the story. To color the story is to add shape and details to what has been said. These details might include more information about a character or a location. To "advance" the story is to say what happens next or add something to the action of the scene.

— *Punctuation Game.* This game requires a few signs, each with a punctuation symbol that is familiar to the class. As the class tells the story, the teacher holds up a sign indicating what item of punctuation their line of the story will end with or indicating that their line of the story is to be followed by quotation marks, a comma, or a colon. Remind students that as they tell the story they are performing. Encourage them to add affect and to play with the rhythm of the lines they deliver. This will help them more fully capture the variations in meaning intended by the particular sign that is guiding their addition to the story.

• *"Yes, but."* This variation of "Yes, and" is often used to illustrate just how important "Yes, and" is in building a scene by demonstrating just how disastrous it is when we intentionally use the word "but" before we add a line. Ironically, leading the class in an intentionally unbuilding activity can work wonders to bring them together. Try it out on a day that your class is having a particularly hard time working together. The game can be played by exactly the same rules as "Yes, and" but with the words, "Yes, but" used to start each sentence instead. Alternatively, a few students can be selected to perform a "Yes, but" scene for the class. They can be given an assignment, such as planning a party for a member of their class, and attempt to complete it with the handicap of starting every sentence with, "Yes, but," which forces them to negate every offer the group makes.

• *Fiction-Style "Yes, and."* Two students are designated as "quote captains." Students tell a story that includes dialogue. When they are saying a line that a character would say, the quote captains stand next to them, using their arms to form open quotes to their right and close quotes to the left of the person who ends the quote.

• *Book Extending "Yes, and."* The class reads a book or short story. Once they have finished, they continue the story together, using "Yes, and," according to what they think might happen next.

Once Upon a Time . . . The End

Improv Level: Intermediate

Grade Level: 2nd grade and up

Time Needed: 30 minutes

Materials: None

This is a unique twist on the collective story format that challenges students to pace themselves so they can set the group up to succeed.

Directions

Five to eight people are chosen to tell a collective story (they may either use the words "Yes, and," or they can be implied). The teacher solicits a first and last line from the class. The first person to speak delivers the first line and the remaining performers continue the story so that the last performer can deliver the last line.

Hints

- If the action of the story progresses too quickly toward the final line, some performers will be left with nothing to say.
- If the story moves off too far away from the final sentence, then the performers will have to work creatively to bring the plot back, so that the final speaker will be able to deliver the final line.

Side Coaching

- "Not too fast. Make sure you leave room for the rest of the performers."
- "Bring the story back so that we can get to the final line."

Extension

- Try choosing a first and last line from a story the class is about to start reading.
- Try choosing the first line from one text and the last line from a different text, where both are drawn from the class's current or prior reading.

I'm Sorry, Did You Say . . . ?

Improv Level: Intermediate

Grade Level: 1st grade and up

Time Needed: 25 minutes

Materials: None

Any teacher of young children can recall a child who loves to talk, plowing ahead with a story regardless of his or her audience's interest. The friendly interruptions in this exercise function as road signs providing subtle redirections to a storyteller that can lead him or her in a new and exciting direction. Because the storyteller never knows when she will be interrupted, the challenge is to think quickly. Stories will quickly be transformed from the banal to the extraordinary.

Directions

Two students sit in front of the class. One student begins telling a story. After a few lines, the second student interrupts, saying, "I'm sorry, did you say . . . ?" indicating disbelief, and then repeats the last word or phrase from the story. The first student then says, "Oh, no, I'm sorry, I meant to say . . . " and then restates the last line, replacing the word or line the other student asked about.

An example might look like this:

Student 1: I had a horrible morning today. My mom forgot to wake me up and I had to walk the dog—

Student 2: I'm sorry, did you say "walk the dog?"

Student 1: Oh, no, I meant to say I had a horrible headache. So I got up and went into the kitchen to get some water—

Student 2: I'm sorry, did you say "get some water?"

Student 1: No, no, I meant I went into the kitchen and slipped on a banana peel. I hit my head and woke up a few hours later in the hospital.

Student 2: I'm sorry, did you say "hospital?"

Student 1: No, I meant to say I woke up on the moon . . .

Hint

- It is better to start with sequential stories, rather than descriptive ones.

Side Coaching

- "Remember, your new word can be completely different from your old one."
- "Be open to going in a completely new direction."
- "Let the story tell itself."

Extension

- After two or three interruptions, have the storyteller pass the story on to a new person. This can either be done arbitrarily, or the storyteller can "write" the new person into the story, for example, "And then I ran into Susan at the bus stop." At this point the storytelling passes to Susan.

Live Action Illustration

Improv Level: Intermediate

Grade Level: All

Time Needed: 30 minutes

Materials: Read-aloud story

For younger students, a favorite part of read-alouds is when the teacher turns the book to reveal the vivid illustrations of the story. In this activity, students become the illustrators. This game is a playful mix of careful listening and fast-paced creativity.

Directions

One student is designated to be the Illustrator and six or seven students are chosen to be the Illustrations. The teacher reads a story, one page at a time. If the story has pictures, the teacher does not show them to the class. At the end of a page, the teacher calls out "Illustrate!" and the Illustrator has 60 seconds to arrange the other children as though they were an illustration for that page. Those students then remain in the front of the room, and the Illustrator rearranges them to make the next picture.

Hints

- Some students will represent characters, while others may represent parts of the setting.
- It is helpful for students who are posing in the Illustrations to remain as the same character throughout the story, with other students added to represent new characters or scenic elements.

Side Coaching

- To the class: "What's missing from the picture?"

Fairy Tale in a Minute

Improv Level: Advanced

Grade Level: 3rd grade and up

Time Needed: 20 minutes

Materials: Hat or bowl, slips of paper, stopwatch

Fairy tales are a wonderful shared cultural experience for many children. Finding details is an important part of developing reading comprehension skills. This exercise puts students under pressure and challenges them to quickly pick the most pithy elements of these stories to present to the class in an often-hilarious, sped-up version of their favorite tales. The spectators will enjoy the comedy of seeing their favorite fairy tales flash before their eyes.

Directions

Fill the hat or bowl with slips of paper with the names of fairy tales or stories that are familiar to the class. These can be written by the teacher or generated by the class by passing out slips of paper on which the students can write the names of their favorite fairy tales.

Three or four students are chosen to perform this scene. One student from each group picks a title out of the hat. The group has 3 minutes to prepare to perform a 1-minute version of their fairy tale. In their brief preperformance discussion, students must decide what the absolutely essential elements are to include in the performance and who will play which parts.

Hint

- If students are struggling, practice dissecting and trimming a fairy tale with the class. Discuss how they might decide which elements are the most critical.

Side Coaching

- "Keep moving!"

Extension

- Have two teams perform the same fairy tale and compare the differences.

The Author Comes to Life

Improv Level: Intermediate

Grade Level: 2nd grade and up

Time Needed: 30 minutes

Materials: None

When students develop a love for a particular author's book, they develop a relationship with that author. Through their stories, students come to know something about who those authors are. In this activity, students can experience what it would be like if their favorite author walked straight into their classroom. This gives them an opportunity to add dimension to the conversations they have been having with and through books and can help develop their enjoyment and understanding of other books by that author.

Directions

One student is chosen to perform as an Author of a book the class has been reading. The students then read a chapter (or the whole book, if it is short) and ask the Author questions about the story. Questions could include when the story was written, what the Author's inspiration was for a character, or why the Author chose to make a particular decision in writing it.

Hints

- Before starting the interview, help the child who is playing the Author think about what her character might be like. What does the Author look like? What might his or her personality be like? Do you think he or she likes children?
- Have children brainstorm questions before starting the interview.

Side Coaching

- "Remember, you don't have to say what the real Author would say. Make something up based on your experience of the Author from having read his/her books."

Extensions

- Have the Author appear in an improv scene with one of the characters from the story.
- Create an improv scene where the Author is one of the characters and appears in an ordinary improv scene set in an ordinary location, such as the laundromat or the playground.

Blah, Blah, Blah

Improv Level: Advanced

Grade Level: 4th grade and up

Time Needed: 30 minutes

Materials: None

This is just an ordinary scene work exercise, with one exception: There are no words! Eliminating words means that students must tune in carefully to the other ways they can receive and express language and be even more attentive to "listening to" offers.

Directions

Two students are chosen to perform in front of the class. They ask the audience for a suggestion of a familiar scene, such as packing up at the end of the day. They then act out the scene saying, "Blah, blah, blah" in place of actual words.

Hints

- Introduce the performers in each scene as you might for any performance, but make your introduction using only "Blah, blah, blah." This will help the performers to embrace the silliness of the scene and to see that even though they are not using words, they can communicate a great deal.
- Encourage students to focus carefully on how their partners deliver their lines and what other gestures or body language are communicated. Then they should respond based on their best guess about what was said. Whether they receive the "correct" message or not is irrelevant because it's the partnership, not the individual speaker, that determines the message.
- Remember, just because there are no words, this does not mean that offers aren't being made that need to be attended to.

Side Coaching

- "Don't try to say everything with hand movements. Listen to what your partner is saying. If you're not sure, make something up and then carefully respond to it."

Extensions

- Find creative opportunities throughout the day to replay a scene using "Blah, blah, blah." A confusing math lesson, a playground squabble, or a funny joke might provide just such an opportunity.
- After doing the exercise, ask students to share what they "heard." Students will delight in hearing everyone's take on what happened, and this replay can become a storytelling exercise in itself.

Boppity, Bop, Bop, Bop

Improv Level: Beginner

Grade Level: 1st grade and up

Time Needed: 10 minutes

Materials: None

Careful listening is critical to learning and to improv. This simple, silly exercise shows just how careful we must be to make sure we are listening and not just reacting.

Directions

Everyone stands in a circle except for one student who is chosen to stand in the middle. This student's objective is to catch one of the other students so as to take his or her place on the outside of the circle. She does this by choosing a student to challenge, approaching him and saying either, "Boppity, bop, bop, bop" or just "Bop." If she says "Boppity, bop, bop, bop," the challenged student must say, "Bop" before she finishes. If she simply says, "Bop," the challenged student is to say nothing. The challenged student is "caught" either if he says, "Bop" when the student in the middle says only "Bop" or if he fails to say, "Bop" before the student in the middle finishes saying, "Boppity, bop, bop, bop."

Hint

- The words "Boppity, bop, bop, bop" can be said quickly but must be stated clearly. Blurring through the words is a tactic that will quickly take the fun out of the game.

Side Coaching

- "Say the words clearly."

Extension

- Make up other silly words and phrases to use in place of "Boppity, bop, bop, bop" or borrow a line from a novel or a play.

Gibberish Poem

Improv Level: Intermediate

Grade Level: 3rd grade and up

Time Needed: 30 minutes

Materials: None

This exercise is a wonderful addition to a poetry unit. As children learn about different styles of poetry and different kinds of rhyming patterns, have them practice making gibberish poems that match the style they're studying. Eliminating real words can help students to perform as poets.

Directions

Choose a style of poetry or rhyming pattern for the class to experiment with. Discuss the elements that are consistent with that style and, if practicing a rhyming pattern, write the pattern where students can see it. Invite students to perform improvised poems for the class that follow that pattern and are spoken in gibberish. An example of a poem following an A-A-B-B rhyming pattern might look like this:

> La blecha la dee de *dom*,
> Gree filla do somily *som*.
> Mee a poo grimenea *leck*,
> Fallala onu gruja *peck*.

Hints

- For young children, it may be necessary to first break it down and do a one-word gibberish rhyming activity first, done in pairs. For example:

  Student A: "dom"
  Student B: "fom"
  Student A: "zom"
  Student B: "krom"

- Add to the reality of the exercise by having the class perform as though the improvising poets were presenting a finished, polished work. Add elements like drums or creative applause where appropriate. Give the audience a performance role, such as an audience at a coffee shop or a group of critics.

Side Coaching

- "Say your poem with passion! Show us that you care about what you're sharing."

Extension

- Try writing improvised song lyrics or jingles designed to sell made-up products.

What's the Meaning of This?

Improv Level: Intermediate

Grade Level: 2nd grade and up

Time Needed: 25 minutes

Materials: Markers and chart paper

Everyone's had the experience of cramming for a vocabulary test or reading an advanced text and coming to a word that is completely incomprehensible. This exercise plays up the comedy of that experience while giving students an opportunity to perform as meaning-makers rather than as simply language users.

Directions

The class is divided into two teams (or many smaller teams). Team #1 makes up a word. The word must be readable and follow the rules of phonics (for example, *quobble* is acceptable but *qdbmn* is not). Team #1 writes the word and the other team (Team #2) then pronounces the word and asks Team #1 to define it and use it in a sentence. Team #1 uses a one-word-at-a-time "Yes, and" format to come up with a definition and a sentence.

With a group of three students, a one-word-at-a-time "Yes, and" recitation for the definition of *quobble* would look like this:

> *Student 1:* Quobble
> *Student 2:* is
> *Student 3:* a
> *Student 1:* word
> *Student 2:* meaning
> *Student 3:* to
> *Student 1:* shout
> *Student 2:* like
> *Student 3:* a
> *Student 1:* gorilla

Hint

- Encourage the team making up the word to perform as though helping the other team study for a vocabulary test.

Side Coaching

- "You're vocabulary experts. Respond with confidence."

Alliteration

Improv Level: Intermediate

Grade Level: 3rd grade and up

Time Needed: 25 minutes

Materials: None

Alliteration exercises will always give an audience ample opportunity for applause. So with this in mind, your students will applaud and laugh hysterically at the ridiculous scenes they create using this literary device.

Directions

Three students are chosen to perform a scene. They are given a setting and a relationship from the audience. They then perform a scene speaking as much as possible in alliteration. For example, the first performer might say, "My mother is the most magnificent mother in all of Missouri." The second performer might reply, "Fine, but my father is far more fabulous."

Hint

- Attempting to make every word or even most words begin with the same letter is not necessary and will likely make the game too challenging. Having even a few words in the sentence is valid alliteration and is still exciting.

Hyperbole

Improv Level: Intermediate

Grade Level: 1st grade and up

Time Needed: 30 minutes

Materials: Chart paper and markers

Nonliteral language such as hyperbole is often difficult for children to understand. This is because it involves the use of (often) absurd situations to make a point stronger, such as how hungry, tall, smart, or fast someone is. Hyperbole in particular is both challenging and excellent fodder for improvisational scenes. As students give shape to these absurd sayings, they will better understand their literary value and the true meaning of exaggeration.

Directions

Discuss the meaning of hyperbole with the class (a figure of speech that is an exaggeration). Brainstorm with the class some examples of hyperbole they are familiar with and invent some of your own. After there is an adequate list, the game begins as students walk freely around the room. After a few moments, call out one of the examples with some context. For example, as students walk around the room, the teacher might call out, "I am so hungry I could eat a horse." Students then act out someone hungrily eating a horse, either as a whole class or in smaller groups. This continues until all of the hyperboles are used.

Hint

- As students create poses together on the spot, encourage them to look out for opportunities to join in with others. For example, if the hyperbole is "taller than a giraffe," a few students might perform as giraffes while another performs as a human towering over them.

Side Coaching

- "Look around at your classmates. What ideas do they have? Whose scene can you join?"

Extension

- Try the exercise again with other examples of nonliteral language such as metaphor and simile.

Read It Again, Sam

Improv Level: Beginner

Grade Level: 2nd grade and up

Time Needed: 30 minutes

Materials: Trade book or textbook

Playing with how we read a text is a fun way to add dimension and character to a student's developing reading performance while transforming dry, monotonous readers into expressive, engaged performers. As readers play with different ways of reading, they build their relationships to the text, supporting the meaning-making process as well as building fluency.

Directions

Choose a short passage from a story or textbook that is at the "just-right" level for the class or reading group. Read the passage once together and then ask for students to volunteer reading the passage again in a different voice or tone. Have several students read the same passage in difference voices.

Here are some possible examples of voices to choose from:

Baby voice	Whisper
Foreign accents	Shouting
Slow motion	Singing
Fast forward	Rapping
Monotone	Scared
TV announcer voice	Excited
High-pitched	Sad
Tired	

Hints

- Don't feel compelled to match a style of reading to the style of the text.
- Encourage students to perform with enthusiasm as they're reading. Add to the theatricality of the exercise by introducing readers as an emcee might.
- Don't be afraid to use this activity when reading about a new topic the class is studying. The performance will help students make meaning out of what they read.

Side Coaching

- "Don't be afraid to act ridiculous!"

Fake It

<table>
<tr><td>

Improv Level: Beginner

Grade Level: All

Time Needed: 25 minutes

Materials: Advanced textbook or trade book

</td></tr>
</table>

Walk into any preschool and you will often see children sitting and "reading" to each other long before they can actually decipher the words on the page. However, by 1st grade children are expected to focus on "real" reading and to stick with books that are appropriate to their ability level. As any literacy course will tell you, reading is about more than deciphering words on a page. "Fake It" brings the fun of performing as a reader back into older children's lives.

Directions

Students are seated as for a guided reading lesson. The teacher distributes copies of a challenging text, one that is too advanced for the students to understand. The students take turns reading a paragraph or a page at a time. For familiar words, they read them as they normally would, but when they come to a word that they don't understand, they "fake it"—making up the sound for the word as though it were entirely familiar. The teacher may pause, as during an ordinary guided reading session, to clarify meaning (even for the words students have faked) or to ask students to make a connection.

Hint:

- Remind students that they are performing as *confident* readers.

Side Coaching

- "If you don't know a word, make it up."
- "Keep your cool. Act like this book is a piece of cake."

Extension

- Try having students read silently from texts that are "too difficult" for them. Have them perform all of their usual silent reading routines such as taking notes, turn-and-talks, asking for help, and completing a reading reflection form. The teacher can also perform her teacher role during these times, moving around the room to monitor reading or working with individual students to "read" with them.

Construct-o-Sentence

Improv Level: Intermediate

Grade Level: 4th grade and up

Time Needed: 25 minutes

Materials: Signs with names of parts of speech, tape or tacks to post signs

Most of us remember learning the parts of speech as a dry, onerous task involving endless memorization and confusing diagrams. With this activity, students can develop their understanding of how various kinds of words fit together while creating silly, offbeat sentences.

Directions

The teacher arranges signs, each with the name of a part of speech, along one wall of the classroom, arranged in an order in which they might be found in a sentence. The teacher then calls children one at a time to stand in front of a sign, left to right, and say a word they want to add to the sentence that is an example of that part of speech. For example, the signs could be arranged: Pronoun, Adverb, Verb, Preposition, Adjective, and Noun. The sentence the students create might then be: "He quickly ran through wet fields."

Hint

- If students are struggling, post a list of common prepositions, pronouns, and adverbs, as those are commonly the most difficult to remember.

Side Coaching

- "Remember, you can use any noun—just think of a person, place, or thing."

Extension

- Once students are confident with the game, have them take charge of placing the parts-of-speech cards. They will quickly learn which combinations result in possible sentences.

Syllable Bingo

Improv Level: Beginner

Grade Level: 1st grade and up

Time Needed: 25 minutes

Materials: None

Learning to recognize individual syllables in words can make decoding and spelling easier. Old-timers will recognize this game from the public television show The Electric Company. *This game, however, has an improvisational twist: Neither performer determines what the word will be—they have to create it together.*

Directions

Students are chosen to compete in teams of two. One team at a time, the students must create words, one syllable at a time. One student says the first syllable, the other says the second, and so on, alternating between the two for each syllable. The words created must be real words. Each word is scored with one point per syllable, so longer words count for more points. If the students are unable to create a word, or if they create a nonsense word, then they receive no points. An example of a three-point word, performed by one team, might look like this:

> *Player A:* car-
> *Player B:* pet-
> *Player A:* ing

Hint

- Remember, a word is not over until neither performer can add on another syllable.

Side Coaching

- "Listen carefully to your partner; his syllable is the offer you build with."
- "Don't think too much. Let the next syllable come to you."
- "Can you make it longer? Is there a way to add a suffix or make it into a compound word?"

Collective Spelling

Improv Level: Beginner

Grade Level: 2nd grade and up

Time Needed: 20 minutes

Materials: Large index cards, a few of them blank and others with the letters of the alphabet on them, including extras of vowels and common letters such as *s, t, n,* and *m.*

For many students, difficulty with spelling can be embarrassing. By turning spelling into a group activity, this embarrassment can be reorganized as a challenge for the whole class. As with "Yes, and," students will be surprised by what they collectively create.

Directions

The class stands in a circle with the index cards spread out in the middle. The first student picks a letter and stands facing the class displaying her letter for everyone to see. The next student stands up and picks a letter that could go next (for example, if the first letter was G the next student might pick an E, but could not pick a T). One by one, students stand up and pick letters until a correctly spelled, complete word emerges (for example, if the next letter chosen was T, the students would have spelled GET).

Hint

* Decide in advance if invented spelling will be allowed.
* Avoid using the exercise as a spelling test.

Side Coaching

* "Think before you pick up a letter. Can the class make a word with those letters?"

Extensions

* Once a word is complete, another student may insert a space so that the next student can begin a new word, allowing the class to create a short phrase or sentence.
* Try the game with words instead of letters, so that students can create whole sentences. Common verbs and articles can be mixed in with vocabulary words or key words from a science lesson.
* Try the game in reverse. Students choose letters at random and stand in a line facing away from the class. On the count of three, they turn to reveal a nonsense word to the class. A volunteer from the class is then chosen to read the word, define it, and use it in a sentence.

Preposition Gymnastics

> **Improv Level:** Intermediate
>
> **Grade Level:** All
>
> **Time Needed:** 25 minutes
>
> **Materials:** Index cards with the names of prepositions

Prepositions link nouns, pronouns, or phrases to other parts of sentences; they establish relationships between people, objects, and ideas. They can be spatial, temporal, or logical. Because prepositions are such tiny words, they are difficult to define, difficult to teach, and, often, difficult to learn, especially for English language learners. This activity allows students to use their bodies to explore the relationships that various prepositions represent.

Directions

This activity has two versions, a beginner version for younger students and an advanced for older ones.

- *Beginner:* The class is divided into two groups. One half is the audience and the other half is given index cards with the names of various spatial prepositions, which they do not show to others in the class, either the audience or one another. When the teacher says, "Go," everyone must quickly move to a spot in the room where their bodies might represent the relationship indicated by their preposition. The teacher then calls, "Freeze," and chooses students in the audience to guess the various relationships that were performed.
- *Advanced:* Two or three students solicit a relationship from the audience; for example, one is an auto mechanic and the other the owner of a broken-down car. Before they begin, each student is given a preposition card. While they act out the scene they must attempt to convey the relationship described by their preposition as part of the action of the scene. They do this by moving around the performance space, adjusting their relationship to their partner or an object in the scene.

Common spatial propositions include: *above, across, along, among, around, at, behind, below, beneath, beside, between, beyond, in, near, under*

Hints

- Several prepositions have similar meanings. Encourage students to be as specific as possible when selecting where to locate themselves. Remind them that they are not trying to trick the audience.
- Suggest to students that they might locate themselves in relationship to one another in addition to objects in the classroom. For example, a student might lean *against* another student who is standing *behind* a desk.

Side Coaching

- "Use the entire space. Think of a creative way to show the audience what preposition you represent."

Extension

- Try adding temporal prepositions, such as *before, after, later,* or *until.*

This Is a What?

Improv Level: Intermediate

Grade Level: 1st grade and up

Time Needed: 25 minutes

Materials: A large bag filled with a variety of objects (at least as many as there are students in the class)

Any teacher will identify with the experience of having several conversations at once. With "This Is a What?," teachers can now share the frustration of that experience with their students. The challenge of this game is in dividing focus between two people without being distracted by the noises and movements of others in the group. Once mastered, students will marvel at their ability to discriminate their focus and manage the chaos.

Directions

The class stands in a circle. One student reaches into the bag and chooses an object without looking—for example, a pen—and turns to the student on his right and says, "This is a pen." The other student says, "A what?" The first replies, "A pen." The second responds, "A what?" The first replies, "A pen," and finally the second student says, "Oh, a pen!" The second student takes the object, turns to her right, and proceeds as before, passing that object on to her right.

At the same time, the first student picks another object from the bag and continues, so that the second student must engage in two conversations at once, turning to the left to say, "A what?" and to the right to answer with the name of the object. This continues until the objects have been passed around the room.

Hints

- If the exercise is difficult at first for the whole class, select a few strong performers to stand in the middle of the circle to demonstrate it for the class. Gradually add more students to the center group until the whole class is involved in the game.
- This game is both simple and very challenging—some groups will not be able to get it right for quite a while.

Side Coaching

- "Remember, you're having a conversation. *Listen* to what your neighbor is saying."

Extensions

- The same exercise is done with an empty bag. Students then remove imaginary objects, which they must name and pass around the circle as above.
- For a very advanced challenge, try the exercise with made-up or gibberish names for the real objects pulled out of the bag. For example, if you pull out a shoe you might say, "A fredge!"

Hot Seat (Literacy Version)

Improv Level: Intermediate

Grade Level: 2nd grade and up

Time Needed: 25 minutes

Materials: 3 chairs

Splitting focus is a skill many teachers have mastered by virtue of much experience with having several conversations and attending to a variety of tasks at once. This exercise allows students a chance to learn how it feels to be in the hot seat, trying to make sense of and participate in two conversations at once, which will undoubtedly improve their listening skills.

Directions

Version 1: Three students sit, shoulder to shoulder, facing the class. The student in the middle is in the Hot Seat. The student to his left begins to engage him in a conversation. After about 30 seconds, the student to his right also begins a conversation with him about an entirely separate topic. The student in the Hot Seat must attempt to participate fully in both conversations, contributing appropriately to each.

Version 2: With this variation, the student in the Hot Seat does not talk, but rather attempts to follow carefully the stories that both students are telling. At the end of the exercise, the student in the Hot Seat must then tell a new story to the class, integrating elements heard in both of the stories he or she was told.

Hints

- Review the basics of having an improvisational conversation. Remind students to try to attend to the offers, however difficult they may be to follow.
- The object of the game is not to try to trip up the student in the Hot Seat. Just as with any improvised scene, everyone's job is to make the ensemble look good.

Side Coaching

- "Listen!"

Extension

- Assign two separate topics that the class has been learning about in school for the students to discuss. Have the student in the Hot Seat tell the class what she learned about the two topics.

Giving Direction

Improv Level: Advanced

Grade Level: 3rd grade and up

Time Needed: 40 minutes

Materials: None

This is a completely ridiculous activity that plays with the fact that we are performing even when we are performing that we are talking about performing (phew!). By placing them in the role of the theatrical director, students can expand their performances as collaborators, uncovering new ideas for communicating, including giving and receiving criticism. Giving and receiving direction turns into an opportunity for saying, "Yes, and" and carefully attending to offers.

Directions

Two students stand in front of the class. One student begins telling a story. After a few moments, the second student interrupts him by saying, "Cut." The second student then gives the first direction on the quality of the presentation, as a director might. For example, the second student might tell the first, "I like that you gave a lot of detail about the toy story. Remember to tell us who the characters are." The first student then interrupts the second, again by saying, "Cut." The first student then critiques the second's performance *of giving directions to her.* Continuing with the above example, the first student might say to the second, "It was helpful that you started by giving me a compliment, and your direction was thoughtful. Perhaps you could say more about 'Tell us who the characters are.'" The game can continue indefinitely with each student giving direction to the other about each student's performance of giving direction.

Hint

- Remember that after the first turn students are giving direction to each other's directions. The initial story is just to get the activity started.

Side Coaching

- "Respond to what your partner *just said.*"

Extension

- Start as above but instead of having students critique one another, have a third student enter after both student #1 and student #2 have a few turns at "Giving Direction." Have student #3 critique both the story and direction offered by student #1 and the direction offered by student #2. After the third student completes her direction, a fourth critiques the performance of the previous three students. The performance continues in a similar fashion with a fifth student and so on, until perhaps the whole class has joined the scene.

Silly Debate

Improv Level: Advanced

Grade Level: 3rd grade and up

Time Needed: 40 minutes

Materials: None

Debate is an ancient ritual that is a part of the traditions of law, science, and academia. Learning to debate involves the skill of persuasion as well as thoughtful listening and responding to what an opposing side is conveying. By experimenting with silly debates, students will have the opportunity to explore the structure of debate without having their interactions determined by truth. With that aspect removed, they are freed to discover elements such as style, timing, and flair.

Directions

Discuss with students the function of a debate. Review the common rules and expectations for a debate, such as each side taking turns, responding to questions from each other and from the audience, and so on. As a class, decide on a silly, meaningless topic to debate, such as whether students should put their left legs or their right legs on top when sitting on the rug. Select teams of students to perform as experts on the topic and stage a debate, complete with opening statements, questions from the floor, and so forth.

Hint

- Encourage students to be passionate about their side, but also to be careful to listen to and respond to what the other side is saying. Remind them that disagreeing is different from negating.

Side Coaching

- "Listen to your opponents. What points are they making? Be sure to respond to what they are saying."

Extension

- After doing the exercise a few times, stage a gibberish debate about a silly topic.

Information Booth

Improv Level: Intermediate

Grade Level: 1st grade and up

Time Needed: 20 minutes

Materials: None

This fast-paced game challenges both the expert and the question-askers to come up with more and more creative questions and answers. It's a fun warmup that can give students the experience of knowing everything and having every question answered.

Directions

One student sits in the Information Booth. Students approach one at a time and ask any kind of question. The Booth's attendant then replies with complete confidence with a completely made-up answer. For example, one student might ask where the shoe department is, another may ask for the square root of 736, another for the capital of Moldova. The information person's answers might be, "Down the hall to the left, 12, and Moldova City," respectively.

Hint

- This game is about creativity and thinking on your feet. It is not about knowing the answers.

Side Coaching

- "Ask anything!"
- "Remember to listen to the question so that your answer is appropriate."

Extension

- Use this game before starting a new unit so that students can ask questions about the topic they are about to study. Then try the exercise again at the end of a unit as an assessment of how much they learned.

Chapter 5

Improvising Mathematics

"I have more than you." "When are we going to get there?" "I am going to need a gazillion blocks." Young children talk math all the time as a natural part of what they're doing. But when children get to school, math quickly becomes separated from what they do; it becomes a subject, a body of knowledge to learn. Too often, when children come to school they stop *doing* math and start *learning* math. Not surprisingly, many children don't make the connection between the math talk in their everyday life and the school subject math. They become alienated from what math is for or even what it is.

Improv can help bring the joy of math back into students' everyday lives. Children can include math in scenes about sports, music, or trips to the amusement park. By playing improv games that include mathematical concepts and problems, children can experience math as a part of ordinary life. The improv activities in this chapter can make the practicality of math more accessible by creating scenes where math is being used, and they also introduce children to the more abstract and philosophical aspects of mathematics. Incorporating math into improv creates an improvisational gym where the class can work out their math muscles.

MATH AS PLAY

Math has an interesting relationship to play. Many people who love math say that they think of it as a game. They love to figure out the rules of the game and play it. They see it as a puzzle or a challenge. On the other hand, those people who don't like math say that there is nothing playful about it. They are often intimidated by its rule-governed nature—that there is only one right answer. These people might argue that math is the opposite of play because in math it is all about getting it right.

Teachers want students to be comfortable with math and at the same time be able to follow very specific rules. Improv provides a way for students to do both. Some of the improv activities in this chapter allow for nonsense and non-truth-driven activities where the goal is to talk and perform as a mathematician. Some of the activities have the rules of mathematics built into the game. In these instances the improv activity is a playful vehicle for memorizing and practicing math skills that can then be used to further develop the class's overall math performance.

Some young children have particular early experiences that support their mathematical development. Playing with numbers, shapes, relationships, and musical rhythms gives children a visceral sense of mathematics. Whether it's because they are already predisposed to think mathematically or they come from families who talk and play this way, there is evidence that these early experiences help shape children's ways of seeing and understanding the world. These children take these early experiences with them into the later grades, and when they encounter more abstract mathematical concepts, they have a way of understanding and making sense of them. Improv can help all children to have experiences where they see, feel, hear, manipulate, and make sense of math. In games such as "Shape Sculpting," "Huggy Bear," and "Upset," children have a multisensory experience of mathematical relationships that does not rely entirely on language, but allows them to experience math in other ways.

As we have said throughout this book, learning requires the organization of environments where people at different levels of development and skill can learn from one another. We believe strongly in group work, so much so that we think much more attention needs to be given to how groups are organized and work together. Given the various relationships people have to math, this is particularly critical. How does one create an environment where students who are afraid of numbers and get butterflies in their stomach at the thought of finding the perimeter of anything can learn from someone who loves nothing better than to multiply fractions? This requires a certain amount of playfulness. When math is incorporated into improv activities, the focus is on the play rather than on the math. In addition, because the activities are rarely competitive, children at different skill levels can participate without some of the fear and embarrassment that come from more competitive games. In activities such as "Math-a-thon" and "Group Juggle," children are competing on behalf of the group instead of individually or against another team. They are struggling to do their best as a group, and this means that children can support and help one another in new ways. Both those children who are great at math and those who struggle have an opportunity to contribute in a way that supports the group's learning.

Learning to do math well requires a certain amount of memorization and rote learning. While it is very important that children understand why $3 \times 4 = 12$, it is also useful to have quick, almost immediate access to basic mathematical facts. Improv games such as "Zip! Zap! Zop!" and "Math-Off" provide playful, improvisational ways to drill math facts.

THE LANGUAGE OF MATHEMATICS

All school subjects have a language—for example, there is a language to history, biology, and literature, as we discuss in Chapter 6. However, there is a particular characteristic to the language of mathematics: In some ways it is a different kind of language. It's a language of logic (what the relationship is between things, not about the things themselves). The 20th-century philosopher Ludwig Wittgenstein talked about how imperfect our languages (English and German, for example) are and how many philosophical muddles are the result of confusions and misperceptions arising from these limitations. Math is an attempt (and a pretty successful one) at writing a pure language, one that conforms to the natural laws of the universe, one that is true a priori. It is a language of precision and rigor. It is the language of facts and their consistent, predictable relationships.

For many children, math is the first introduction to this kind of discourse, one in which getting it exactly right is what is demanded. Some children love and thrive on the precision; others hate it and become confused and lost. With improv there is an opportunity for everyone to perform the language of mathematics. In games like "Jargon" children include math language in their improv scenes without being afraid of getting the answers wrong, while in activities like "Captain Precision" they can play with the need to get answers exactly right.

While math is used to describe relationships in the natural world, it is still, like literature and theater, created by actual people. All the algorithms, formulas, and theorems; all the names of the shapes and systems for measuring, comparing, sorting, and classifying were created by people to help describe relationships in the world. Like its cousins in the sciences, the language of mathematics has been enormously successful in helping human beings make new discoveries and inventions, and it's a language that continues to grow by virtue of people playing and experimenting with new ways of seeing and understanding those relationships.

In part because math is so precise and truth-governed, children do not think of it as having been created by human beings, and therefore they do not see themselves as having an active relationship to what they are learning. Children are not alone in this. Most adults see mathematical knowledge as being a part of the natural order of things. Improv, because it is about creating rather than acquiring knowledge, has the potential to connect children to the creative process by which human beings give rise to mathematical knowledge. The improv activities in this chapter give children an opportunity to play with and make up new mathematical concepts and words and to experiment with a variety of ways of seeing and explaining mathematical relationships between things in the world.

CREATING MATH PERFORMANCES

There is, in addition to the language of mathematics, a performance to being a mathematician. Unfortunately, in our current culture it is not a performance to be imitated. The stereotype of the math person is not particularly positive and is definitely not cool. The popular culture image of a mathematician or a good math student is someone who is always logical and precise and sees everything in terms of numbers or formulas. He is someone who carries a ruler around in his shirt pocket or pencil bag, has a calculator in hand, and is awkward when talking to people—in short, a nerd. These stereotypes can limit children's willingness to explore particular careers and can keep certain other children isolated from the rest of the class. In improv children create new performances and characters of people who love or are good at math. They can create the "Cool Math Guy" or the "Hilarious Math Girl" as characters in their scenes. The class can create a culture where doing math is a valued performance.

Improv provides a way to play with and explore some of the subjective experiences people have when learning math. For some students and teachers seeing numbers or shapes on a page elicits panic and confusion that prevents them from even attempting to solve the problem. As we have said before, improv does not separate the affective aspects of learning from the cognitive. In activities such as "Emotional Math Class" and "'I'm Sorry, Can You Explain That Another Way?," the class can try on different emotional responses to actual math problems. We have found that including the emotional experience students are having when learning math can make the difference between a failing class and a successful class.

Math experts agree that a critical part of learning math is not only being able to get the right answer, but being able to understand and explain how the answer was arrived at. While this is obviously a conceptual issue and requires lots of experience and practice, in our experience it is also helped by imagination and creativity. Improv can provide a means of helping children philosophize about what they are learning and find creative ways to describe their nascent mathematical understandings. For example, small groups of children can create scenes for explaining what happens when doing two-digit subtraction that requires "borrowing." Improv provides a tool for helping children share how they solved problems and improvise new ways of solving problems.

IMPROVISING MATHEMATICAL CONVERSATIONS

We want to conclude this chapter with a personal story from Carrie's first year as an early childhood teacher because we think it might help other teachers be more creative and think outside the box about both improv and math.

When I (Carrie) first started teaching I was definitely not a math person. Thankfully, from my perspective at the time, my liberal arts college had not required me to take any math classes, so the last time I tackled the subject was in 11th grade. In my family my sister was the math person; I loved words. When I became a preschool teacher I discovered that the children could compete over anything—who had more crackers, who could climb the highest, how old they were, how many Ninja Turtle toys they owned. In the beginning I responded to these conversations behaviorally—if they led to fights or loud arguments I would intervene and talk about the issue from a social perspective, and if they didn't, I ignored them.

After a few of years of teaching I started taking classes in improv and, as is evidenced by this book, it has a profound impact on my teaching. One of the most surprising changes was in my relationship to math and to teaching math. As I began to improvise more with the class, I heard the children's arguments about size, age, and quantity as offers to do math together. We began to create math games and conversations that had their origins in the children's endless discussions about who was bigger, taller, and faster. One of our favorite creations was "Can You Beat That Number?" In this game show activity one child would call out a number and I would say, "Who can beat that number?" Another child would then have to say a higher number. For example, if the first child said 6, the next child might say 10. If the second child said 5, I would say, "Too low, who can beat that number?" We created other performances, including "Too Many, Too Few," "Which Is Bigger?," and "How Far Can We Stretch?" We learned how to play with math together. One day in the teacher lunch room I overheard a colleague talking about me to someone else and she said, "Well, Carrie loves math." I almost fell out of my chair. But she was right. By playing and improvising with numbers and shapes with the children I was teaching, I had become someone who saw the world mathematically and had grown to love it.

The readers of this book are sure to run the gamut from math lovers to those who are math-phobic. One concern is that teachers who are themselves afraid or lack confidence in their math abilities can produce a vicious cycle of children mislearning or learning to fear the subject. The activities in this chapter are designed to get everyone started improvising with math, whatever their previous history or experience. In addition to using the activities we supply, we also hope that you and your students will be inspired to find new and improvisational ways to create mathematical conversations and activities with and between students, just as Carrie invented with hers.

Compulsive Math Gal/Guy

Improv Level: Intermediate

Grade Level: 2nd grade and up

Time Needed: 20 minutes

Materials: None

Everyone is familiar with the stereotype of someone who is a compulsive student of math. Often this level of excitement about math is seen as one and the same as being a geek or nerd. In this exercise, students can try out the performance of being enthralled with math, regardless of their actual level of competence or even interest in the subject. As they do so, they can create new performances and, as a result, new associations with what a math fanatic might be like.

Directions

Two students are chosen to perform in a scene. They ask the class for a location where two people might be having a conversation. One student is designated as the Compulsive Math Gal/Guy. He or she is completely obsessive about math and attempts to make every conversation mathematical. As the two perform the scene, the other student works to build with the that offers the Compulsive Math Gal/Guy is making, but is not necessarily thrilled to have every element of the conversation be about math.

Hint

- The student who is not the Compulsive Math Gal/Guy is responsible for taking extra care in building with offers and moving the scene along.

Side Coaching

- "Make every single sentence about math."

Extension

- Find moments when the Compulsive Math Gal/Guy can appear throughout the day.

Captain Precision

Improv Level: Intermediate

Grade Level: 1st grade and up

Time Needed: 20 minutes

Materials: Cape or wand with a large *P*

Captain Precision is no ordinary superhero. Instead of merely saving busloads of tourists or damsels in distress, he or she rescues conventional conversations from their vague inaccuracies, bringing meticulous precision to the far reaches of the universe. As they create their own "Captain Precision" performances, students will explore the language of precision that characterizes mathematics.

Directions

Two students volunteer to begin a scene. They solicit a suggestion from the audience for who they are and a location where they might run into one another. They begin the scene, and after about 2 minutes, a third student, designated as Captain Precision, enters the scene with the gusto of a superhero. The job of Captain Precision is to ask questions or "correct" the dialogue of each of the other students to make it more precise. For example, one student may be describing a humorous event that took place the previous day involving a trash can that she accidentally turned over. Captain Precision insists that she say at precisely what time the incident took place and the velocity at which the trash can fell over, and detail each of its contents.

Hint

- Demonstrate and brainstorm with your students examples of precise and imprecise language.

Side Coaching

- To Captain Precision: "Ask for more. Insist that they give you every detail."

Extension

- As with Compulsive Math Gal/Guy, Captain Precision can make surprise visits at any time of day, such as during a social studies lesson, in the cafeteria, or during gym class.

Emotional Math Class

Improv Level: Beginner

Grade Level: All

Time Needed: 30 minutes

Materials: None

Let's face it, math can be one of the most emotional times of day for some students—and teachers. Even young students begin the school year with a host of prior experiences with math, and for many of them, these experiences were difficult. In this exercise, everyone has the opportunity to explore and create with his or her emotional responses to math.

Directions

Students are seated on the rug or at their desks as for a regular math lesson. One student is designated the Emotions Captain. Every few minutes, while the teacher is delivering a regular math lesson, the Emotions Captain calls out an emotion for the class (including the teacher) to incorporate into the lesson, such as sad, angry, confident, jealous, or terrified.

Hint

- Remember that this is a real math lesson. It is more challenging to perform these emotions when attending to the various responsibilities of teaching and participating in a math lesson, but that adds to the significance of the scene.

"I'm Sorry, Can You Explain That Another Way?"

Improv Level: Intermediate

Grade Level: 1st grade and up

Time Needed: 25 minutes

Materials: Math book

Whenever teaching a new math skill, it is inevitable that a few students will get it quickly and others will require additional explanation. It is an all-too-common experience for everyone involved—the student, the other students in the class, and even the teacher—to get frustrated with trying to grasp or explain a problem in words that are understandable. This exercise is a mathematical version of "I'm Sorry, Did You Say . . . " in which students can create new experiences with explaining and teaching math.

Directions

Two students are chosen to perform this exercise. They sit in two chairs facing the audience. Student A is attempting to explain to student B how to complete a particular math problem or exercise. After student A explains a few steps, student B interrupts, saying, "I'm sorry, could you explain that another way?" And then student A must go back, explain it differently, and proceed until interrupted again.

Hint

- The object is not for student A to arrive at the perfect way of explaining the problem. Allow students to expand their skill and vocabulary through finding new and creative ways of explaining.

Side Coaching

- "What are some other words you could use to explain the problem?"
- "Try drawing a picture."

Jargon

Improv Level: Intermediate

Grade Level: 2nd grade and up

Time Needed: 20 minutes

Materials: Fish bowl filled with slips of paper with math words or phrases that are unfamiliar to the class

Beginning a new math unit can often feel like taking a plunge into a mathematical alphabet soup. As math gets more complex, new vocabulary is less familiar because it is less a part of daily life. This activity gives students an opportunity to get the feel for the math language they will encounter in a few days or even a few years.

Directions

Two or three students are chosen to begin a scene that takes place in a location chosen by the audience. After the scene gets started, the teacher hands one student a slip of paper from the fish bowl. The student must then incorporate that word into his next line of dialogue in the scene.

Hint

• With longer words, read through the list of terms before playing.

Side Coaching

• "Remember, you don't have to know what the word means. Make something up."

Mathematical "Yes, and"

> **Improv Level:** Intermediate
>
> **Grade Level:** 2nd grade and up
>
> **Time Needed:** 20 minutes
>
> **Materials:** Three small signs, one each with "+," "−," and "="

This "Yes, and" extension brings a mathematical twist to the improv stalwart.

Directions

Students sit in a circle as they would for the original version of "Yes, and." They are to tell a story, one sentence at a time, beginning each sentence with the words "Yes, and." Between each student's turn, the teacher holds up a " + ," " −," or " = " sign. This indicates to the next student that the number of characters in the scene should increase, decrease, or stay the same. Once students have mastered the game, a student can take over the task of holding up the signs.

Hint

- This format is ripe for creating absurd stories. Resist the urge to moderate this by overusing the " = " sign.

Side Coaching

- "Remember, we're still looking out for offers, and still working to build with them."

Extension

- Instead of simply increasing or decreasing the number of characters in the story, tell students to increase or decrease by a particular number, for example, holding up the "−" sign and saying "two," indicating that the number of characters in the story should decrease by two.

Word Problems Come to Life (and Get Out of Control)

Improv Level: Beginner

Grade Level: All

Time Needed: 20–30 minutes

Materials: Math textbooks or workbooks with word problems; deck of index cards with a range of numbers (large and small, including decimals or fractions if appropriate) written on them

Word problems can too often become exercises in translating words into mathematical language. Inexperienced students may scan the problems for numbers, make a guess at the operation they are to use, and compute an answer without understanding the meaning of the problem. Bringing the problems to life and playing around with the mathematical content will allow children to develop a deeper understanding of the problems.

Directions

Select a word problem of the kind the class is working on. Write the problem on the board with a blank space in place of all the numbers. Select students to perform a scene that will include the word problem. For example, if Johnny is buying apples in the problem, cast a student to play Johnny and another to play the grocer. Before the scene begins, choose a card or cards from the deck to tape in place of the numbers in the word problem. After students perform the scene, the audience must give the answer to the problem by solving the problem and, as in all word problems, stating it in a complete sentence. The scene is then performed again with the same word problem but with new numbers selected in place of the first. Because these numbers can vary greatly in magnitude, the performances will vary accordingly.

Hints

- Encourage students to embellish stories that lack flourish, as long as they don't change the math.
- Remind the children in advance to think about how the size of the numbers may vary their performances.

Side Coaching

- "You just asked for eight thousand apples. How are you going to carry them?"
- "She just ordered one-sixth of an apple. Find a knife."

Extension

- Have students write their own out-of-this-world story problems with unlikely numbers for the class to perform.

Improvisational Word Problem

Improv Level: Intermediate

Grade Level: 2nd grade and up

Time Needed: 20–30 minutes

Materials: None

Students often struggle with the language and format of word problems. Some of them are able to solve them only by seeking out certain key words that tell them what operation to plug in. With this activity, students can create their own word problems on their feet, acting out real-life scenes so that they can create, see, hear, and feel the elements of the problem.

Directions

Three students are chosen to begin a scene. The teacher has written an equation on the board, such as $43 - 15 = $ ___. The students ask for a location from the audience where their scene is taking place. They must then create a live-action word problem that uses the equation the teacher has given them to make a word problem. For example, with the equation $43 - 15 = $ ___, the students might create a scene where a squirrel spends hours and hours gathering nuts, only to have an evil rat steal 15 of them. The scene ends with the performers asking a question of the audience, similar to the last line in a word problem that requires them to solve the problem. In the case of the problem above, the question might be: "How many nuts did she have left?" The audience then gives their solution to the problem and the performers end the scene.

Hint

- Encourage students to be attentive to both the math task and the creation of the scene using "Yes, and."

We Are a Square

Improv Level: Beginner

Grade Level: All

Time Needed: 25 minutes

Materials: None

In this game, students create geometric shapes on the go, using their entire bodies. They also have the opportunity to challenge their fellow students by calling out shapes the class may be less familiar with.

Directions

Students stand in a circle. At any moment, one student may enter the circle and call out, "I am a . . . " and then say the name of a geometric shape known to the class. For younger kids, these might include a triangle, a circle, and a rectangle. With older kids, students might call out "scalene triangle" or "hectogram." That first student then poses, either standing up or lying down, as one part of that shape. Subsequent students then join in, one at a time, to collectively complete the figure, each one representing a part of the entire shape. When the shape is complete, the first student selects all but one student to leave the center of the circle, leaving that student to begin the next shape.

Hint

- Consider playing "I Am a Tree" from the science section of Chapter 6 as a warmup.

Extension

- Add another element to the activity by asking students to factor in their various heights as they decide which students should join in, to make each element of the shape they produce have the correct dimensions.

Shape Sculpting

Improv Level: Beginner

Grade Level: All

Time Needed: 20 minutes

Materials: None

Whether it's squares and circles in kindergarten or heptagons and pyramids in 5th grade, math is filled with shapes that students need to become familiar with. With "Shape Sculpting," students carefully craft the shapes they're studying with their own and their class's imaginations.

Directions

Everyone sits in a circle. The teacher makes a list of shapes the students are familiar with. With younger children, these will likely be only two-dimensional objects, but with older children three-dimensional objects may be used. One student begins by carefully molding a shape out of imaginary clay, facing the student to his left. He should take the time and care to form the object using his hands or imaginary tools so that the person to his left will be able to name the shape of the object. If she cannot, then the clay is smashed back together and he tries again.

Hints

- Some younger children may not be able to make the shapes with their hands; this activity will work only once they have developed the eye–hand coordination.
- For two-dimensional objects, remind students that they will need to flatten the "clay" by pressing it down or using an imaginary rolling pin to flatten it out. Model this carefully for younger students.
- Make a list of shapes that are fair game for the activity. This will limit guessing and encourage students to challenge themselves.

Side Coaching

- "Go slowly. Take us carefully through each step in your process."

Human Balance

Improv Level: Intermediate

Grade Level: 3rd grade and up

Time Needed: 20 minutes

Materials: Masking tape

Symmetry is a key concept in elementary mathematics. This exercise is an advanced version of "Mirrors" that turns a classroom into a human balance beam where students can create life-sized symmetrical scenes with their own bodies.

Directions

The performance space is divided into two halves by a straight line made with tape or designated with cones. The class is told that the line represents the center point of a balance. Two performers are chosen and designated as A and B. They stand on opposite sides of the line, equally distant from the center line. A is designated as the leader and B must mirror his movements exactly. If A moves away from the line, B must move the same distance away. If A moves to the right, B moves to the left. If A jumps up and down and sticks out her tongue, B must do the same. At all times, the objective is to maintain perfect balance. Add a second and then a third pair of students to join the scene, partnered with one another on opposite sides of the line. Encourage the A's on the same side to interact while the B's interact in exactly the same manner. After switching leadership between the A's and B's, announce that no one is leading and that each side must carefully work together to create leaderless, fluid movement around the space.

Hints

- This activity is best done in a large, empty space. If your classroom is small and it is not easy to move furniture out of the way, consider using a gym, dance studio, or wide hallway.
- Introduce this activity to the class after practicing "Mirrors" a few times. This will allow students to practice matching body movements.
- As with "Mirrors," the objective is not for one person to trick the other. Instruct the students to be attentive to whether or not their partner is with them and make adjustments accordingly.

Side Coaching

- "Remember, you're mirroring. If your partner moves her left arm, you'll move your right."
- "Copy *everything* your partner is doing. Notice their facial expressions. Notice their breathing. How are their fingers arranged?"

Extension

- Execute a two-person scene where the two performers must work through a dialogue while maintaining perfect symmetry with their scene partner's movements.

Expanding Cast

Improv Level: Intermediate

Grade Level: All

Time Needed: 20 minutes

Materials: None

One of the best ways to help children develop number sense is to get them on their feet and let them actually experience changing numbers. In this activity, the numbers grow and grow until they reach absurdity.

Directions

One student is chosen to begin a scene in a location determined by the class. The teacher then calls out a multiple and the scene is replayed with the number of students in the scene increased by that multiple. For example, if one student is performing brushing his teeth in the bathroom and the teacher calls out "Four!," three new students join the scene, so that there are a total of four students brushing their teeth ($1 \times 4 = 4$). The teacher then continues to call out multiples until everyone in the class is performing in the scene. If the above scene were to continue and the teacher called out "Three!," then 8 more students would join the scene to make a total of 12 ($4 \times 3 = 12$).

Hint

- Encourage students to choose locations and activities that would be especially absurd if they involved large numbers of people, for example the back seat of a hatchback, a walk-in freezer, or a closet.

Side Coaching

- "Remember, you're all crammed into the bathroom together. What might make that difficult? What would the conversation look like?"

Half the Time

Improv Level: Advanced

Grade Level: 3rd grade and up

Time Needed: 25 minutes

Materials: Stopwatch

Anyone who has taught young children has had to explain how long a particular amount of time is ("We're going to lunch in five minutes. That's about how long it takes you to walk to the gym and back.") This activity provides children with a fun way to explore how long various activities take, thus expanding their familiarity with different measures of time. It also provides a hands-on activity for teaching the concept of one-half.

Directions

Three performers are chosen to create a short scene. While they perform the scene, another student, the timekeeper, times the scene with a stopwatch. The performers must then act out the exact same scene a second time, only this time they must perform it in exactly half the time. This continues with the same scene getting cut in half again and again until the scene because absurdly short.

Hints

- During the second and third performances of the scene, have the timekeeper let the performers know when they have 1 minute left, and then again when there are 15 seconds remaining, so the performers can pace themselves.
- Guide the students in focusing carefully on the essential elements of the scene. The elements that are not essential to the action can be cut to save time.

Side Coaching

- "Keep moving! Try to cover just the most important elements."

Time of Your Life

Improv Level: Intermediate

Grade Level: 1st grade and up

Time Needed: 30 minutes

Materials: Blank index cards, tape or thumbtacks

Children's lives, both inside and outside the classroom, are filled with routines. In fact, good teachers are known for establishing predictable, patterned routines. In this activity, children play around with those routines to further their understanding of sequence, an important component of the elementary mathematics curriculum.

Directions

The class brainstorms a list of activities they ordinarily complete in a regular, particular sequence during the course of the day, for example, finishing social studies, putting their social studies books away, lining up for gym, walking to gym class, and then playing basketball in the gym. Five activities are selected, written on large index cards, and posted in chronological order in the front of the classroom. The students then create a scene in which each of those five tasks is completed. Once they are finished, the cards are shuffled and displayed again in a new, perhaps illogical order for the students to perform again.

Hint

- Some of the tasks will likely be absurd in a particular order, such as walking to gym class before they have lined up. Remind the students to acknowledge and justify that absurdity in their performances.

Side Coaching

- "Wait, you're feeding the dog, but you're already at school. Share with us how the dog got to school."

Extension

- Surprise your students after they've completed a typical classroom routine. Write on the board the sequence of steps they completed as part of the routine and then have them perform the routine again with the same steps in a new order.

Attributes

Improv Level: Beginner

Grade Level: All

Time Needed: 15 minutes

Materials: None

Sorting, describing, and categorizing are important emergent mathematical tasks and a precursor to the skills of algebra. The idea that some objects have several characteristics and have a variety of things in common is made apparent in this fun activity. Students will be surprised to learn what they have in common that is not at first apparent.

Directions

Everyone stands in a circle except for one student, who stands in the middle. That student begins by saying something about herself. For example, she might say, "I have a blue backpack." Each student who has that characteristic must switch places with another student who shares it. The student in the middle then races to one of the empty spots, attempting to get there before another student, so as not to be left in the middle. Whoever is left in the middle then says something about him- or herself, and the game continues.

Hints

- Consider excluding physical descriptions once students have played a few times. This will challenge students to think of less obvious characteristics to identify.
- Make sure to arrange students in the circle so that it will be clear where each empty space is.

Side Coaching

- "Think of something you've always wondered about your classmates."

Extension

- With older kids, try calling out two categories. For example, "I love my neighbor who has a cat *and* who comes to school on the bus." Only students who fit both characteristics will leave the circle.

Group Juggle

Improv Level: Beginner
Grade Level: 1st grade and up
Time Needed: 10 minutes
Materials: A soft, small ball that is easy to catch

Patterns exist everywhere in our lives. With this activity, students have the chance to create and re-create a pattern. This activity can also be used as a fun way to kick off a math lesson, or a quick activity the class can play while waiting for the bus.

Directions

The students spread out around the room. The teacher begins by tossing a ball to one student. That student then passes the ball on to another student. Once the student passes the ball, she places a hand on her head to indicate to everyone else that she has already received the ball and no one should throw it to her again. This continues until everyone has received the ball, and finally it is thrown back to the teacher. The ball is then tossed a second time, with the students challenged to repeat the pattern exactly as before. Finally, in the third round, the ball is not passed but instead students pretend they are throwing a ball.

Hint

- Remind students that they only need to remember who passes them the ball and who they pass it to.

Side Coaching

- "Remember who passed you the ball and who you have to pass it to."

Extensions

- Try the exercise a fourth time in reverse order.
- Once students have mastered this, try adding a second or even a third ball in reverse.

Huggy Bear/Buddy Up!

Improv Level: Beginner

Grade Level: All

Time Needed: 10 minutes

Materials: None

This is an excellent activity for practicing one-to-one correspondence with younger children and introducing the concept of division and remainders to older students. Unlike grouping beads or pennies, however, students get to group themselves.

Directions

Students spread out around the room. The teacher begins by calling out "Huggy bear!" (or "Buddy up!" for older students) and then a number. The students then join together in groups of that number and "hug" together. For example, if the teacher calls out "Huggy bear three," students must hug as groups of three. With some numbers, of course, there will be students left over, and with others there may be even groups.

Hints

- Be clear ahead of time about whether the teacher or other adults are participating, as this will affect the number of students who will be left over for various numbers.
- Once they've played a few times, older students can be challenged to guess how many will be left over for each number.
- End the game by calling out "Huggy bear . . ." and then the total number of students in the class. This will bring everyone together and set up your class to move on to the next activity.

Side Coaching

- "How many students do you think will be left over? Why?"

Extension

- Try calling out math problems, such as, "Buddy up seven minus four" or "Buddy up the square root of nine."

Mingle

Improv Level: Beginner

Grade Level: All

Time Needed: 15 minutes

Materials: None

Sorting objects into categories is an important math skill. This fun and easy activity may challenge students' notions about what they have in common with various classmates and provide an opportunity for everyone to learn something new about one another.

Directions

Students move freely around the room. After a few minutes the teacher calls out the name of a category, such as "everyone who has a pet." All the students who fit into that category must quickly find one another and stand together in a group. Once the class has done the activity a few times, designate a student as the Category Caller.

Hint

- Challenge students to think beyond obvious, physical characteristics, including such characteristics as where they are from, interests, ethnicity, favorite/least favorite foods, and so on.

Extension

- Have students take turns leading the game, inventing new and unusual characteristics.

Pattern Dance

Improv Level: Beginner

Grade Level: All

Time Needed: 20 minutes

Materials: None

Young children love spotting patterns. As they enter school, patterns become a part of the math curriculum, as identifying and forming patterns is an important component of arithmetic. Creating patterns socially is a fun way to practice this skill. In version three, we've thrown in an improvisational twist: Students will have to think about patterns in more complex ways as they look for and build with their classmates' offers.

Directions

Version One: The teacher assigns a pattern for half of the students in the class without telling the other half what the pattern is. If the pattern is AABB, for example, the students then line up with some movement or physical characteristic representing that pattern. They could choose to line up boy-boy-girl-girl, they could roll up left sleeves and right sleeves, they make two distinct noises, and so forth. The class must then guess the pattern.

Version Two: After practicing a few times, have students huddle together and choose their own pattern.

Version Three: Older students can create a pattern as they go without first determining the pattern as a group. For example, an impromptu ABCABC pattern might look like this:

1. Raises left arm (A)
2. Pulls on ear (B)
3. Jumps up and down (C)
4. Raises left arm (A)
5. Pulls on ear (B)
6. Jumps up and down (C)

Hint

- Remind students that the third version of this activity is similar to "Yes, and" in that it is the group, and not any individual, that determines the pattern. They must be attentive to the offers of the group.

Side Coaching

- "Remember, the pattern you have in mind to begin with might not be the one your classmates make."

Upset

Improv Level: Beginner

Grade Level: 2nd grade and up

Time Needed: 20 minutes

Materials: None

This activity is a fun challenge involving the whole class. Once introduced, it can be used as frequently as possible for a quick and fun way of lining up. The rules can be altered as needed, and there are endless possibilities to keep students on their toes.

Directions

The class stands in a large circle. Students are told that when the teacher calls out "Upset," they will need to arrange themselves in the circle according to the date and month of their birthdays, so that someone with a January 4 birthday would line up in front of someone with a January 18 birthday and so on. The teacher should tell students where the person with the first birthday should stand, then where the second should stand, and so on. The teacher then calls out "Upset!" and the class quickly moves to their spots while the teacher times them.

Students are instructed to remember the order they are in, and then a second characteristic is chosen, such as arranging themselves alphabetically according to the letters in their name.

With older students, a third category can be introduced, such as height. The teacher then calls out different categories, such as "Birthdays, upset!" As the exercise goes on, the teacher challenges students to line up in less and less time.

Hint

- Perfection is not the goal, and the activity is most successful when students are encouraged to fake it even if they have not quite got it right.

Side Coaching

- "Okay, time's up. Even if you're not in the right spot, pretend you are. Act cool!"

Extensions

- Once they've attempted the exercise a few times, challenge the students to complete it silently.
- Instead of arranging themselves in a circle, students can line up in a straight line as they would to move to another part of the school. This challenge works especially well when timed and when completed without talking.
- Keep track of how fast students are able to get lined up, and post a graph of those times in the classroom.

Place Value Game

Improv Level: Beginner

Grade Level: 2nd grade and up

Time Needed: 20 minutes

Materials: Large signs with the words "Ones," "Tens," "Hundreds," etc.

Understanding place value is a critical step for moving from basic numeracy into computation. With this activity, students can explore with their bodies the very different values created when digits are moved from one place-value column to another.

Directions

Signs with the names of various place values are laid out on the floor with the larger values to the left descending to the right. For example, a sign saying "thousands" would be on the left, and to the right "hundreds," then "tens," and finally, "ones." One student is designated as the Counter and the rest are the Digits. When the teacher calls, "Go!" the Digits must each quickly line up behind one of the place-value signs, forming a column with each student representing one part of the number. Once everyone is lined up, the teacher calls "Freeze!," and the Counter must call out the number that the class has created. This is done by counting the number of students in each column; if there are 4 students in the thousands column, 2 students in the hundreds column, 7 in the tens column, and 8 in the ones column, then the number is 4,278. The game can then be played in reverse, with the teacher calling out a number for the class to form and designating a place for extra Digits to gather.

Hints

- Remind students that there cannot be more than nine of them in any given column. If more than nine line up, the extras will need to move to another column.
- With younger students, consider teaching a lesson on place value that uses columns of dots in addition to integers to help them see the one-to-one relationship highlighted in this game.

Side Coaching

- "Okay, tens column. There are more than nine of you, so you are full."
- "What's the biggest four-digit number we can make using everyone in the class?"

Extension

- Extend the game to an adding game, where two sets of columns are formed facing each other. When the columns are added, some numbers may need to be carried.

Odds or Evens

Improv Level: Intermediate

Grade Level: 2nd grade and up

Time Needed: 30 minutes

Materials: None

This game is a sort of mathematical Odd Couple. *Mastering odd and even numbers can help students make basic computations more quickly, recognize errors, and develop their mathematical sense. The extension, which adds the component of character, allows students to create connections between the personality characteristics of being odd- or even-headed, and the mathematical meanings of those words.*

Directions

Two students are chosen to perform a scene. They are given a setting and a relationship from the audience that will help them to create a scene where they use lots of numbers (for example, they are cashiers at a store). One student is Odd and the other is Even. When they discuss numbers (which they should do often), Even can only mention even numbers and Odd can only mention odd numbers. A scene might look like this:

Even: Those two candy bars cost exactly *forty* cents each. Kindly be sure to attach the price tags properly.
Odd: You think you're the *only one* who can put the prices on?
Even: I apologize if I've offended you, Odd. I have worked here for *six* months now.
Odd: I brought *five* peanut butter and potato sandwiches for lunch.
Even: Well, you can eat your lunch break at *twelve* o'clock.

Hints

- Remind students to create scenes where they can use lots of numbers.
- For younger students, review odd and even numbers before playing or write them on the board for their references. Assign an audience member as Number Judge to keep an eye out for mistakes.
- Watch out for common phrases that include numbers but might not be recognized, such as "One time I . . ." They still count.

Side Coaching

- "Remember, while you're trying to include numbers, also keep the scene moving."

Extensions

- Try the scene adding a unique personality to each character. Odd is an odd person who's messy and acts and speaks strangely; Even is level-headed, thoughtful in her speech, and clear and rational.
- An advanced version of the game could include other math facts in place of odd and even numbers, for example, prime and composite. Students can also complete simple math problems back and forth. In this case, the teacher chooses an operation and each student says a number that gets added to the equation.

Math-a-Thon

Improv Level: Intermediate

Grade Level: 2nd grade and up

Time Needed: 25 minutes

Materials: None

This game moves math problems out of your students' heads and brings them into the classroom. As they improvise math problems together, they will develop their skills at solving problems as a group. Doing so will help them (and you) discover ways of making use of the different skill levels in the class.

Directions

Version One: The class sits in a circle. Moving clockwise around the circle, one student at a time, the class makes up and solves math problems. Each person says a number, an operation, or "equals," depending on where they are in the sequence. A problem might look like this:

1st Student: Seven
2nd Student: Plus
3rd Student: Twelve
4th Student: Equals
5th Student: Nineteen

Once the problem is complete, the next student in the circle then starts a new one by calling out a new number.

Version Two: Once the students are comfortable with Version One, they can create longer problems where more than two numbers are added, subtracted, multiplied, or divided. The problem keeps getting larger until one student calls out "equals," and then the next person must say the answer.

Hints

- For Version Two, coach students to be thoughtful about when they call out "equals." If they want to push themselves, they may take pride in letting the equation grow longer or using more difficult operations.
- When playing Version Two, keep track of the numbers and operations on the board so that the group can check their answer.
- Be creative about how you make use of students who are relatively better or worse at keeping track of numbers in their heads. For example, one student might serve as a roving helper, keep track of numbers on the board, or assist with an "instant replay" that students can use to help them backtrack to solve the problem.
- Remind students that with this exercise, as in all improv games, the object is to *make the group look good*. Setting each other up or becoming competitive is at odds with this objective.

Side Coaching

- "Everyone should keep track of the problem in his or her head because you never know when someone might call 'equals.'"

Math-Off

Improv Level: Intermediate

Grade Level: 2nd grade and up

Time Needed: 25 minutes

Materials: None

Teachers have always used some kind of drill format to prac-tice math problems. This exercise adds an improvisational twist that makes practicing math problems more social and more playful.

Directions

Version 1: The class forms two parallel lines (Line A and Line B), standing back to back, as though lining up for a drill in gym class. Before the exercise, the teacher announces to the class what operation they will be practicing (addition, multiplication, etc.). The two students in the front of each line begin with the person from Line A saying a number, the person from Line B another number, and then the Line A person completes the equation based on the operation given by the teacher. The student from Line A then moves to the end of Line B and the student from Line B moves to the end of Line A.

Version 2: Students line up as in Version 1. This time the audience calls out a location and the pair must exchange three lines of dialogue that might be heard at that location, but that also include a number. The third number stated in the dialogue is the solution to the problem based on the operation given by the teacher. For example, if someone in the class calls out "a diner" and the operation is multiplication, the dialogue might go like this:

> *A:* Can I borrow three dollars?
> *B:* I don't get paid for another two weeks.
> *A:* I'm not sure how I'm going to pay for the six hamburgers I just ate.

Hint

- Once you've practiced Version 1 several times, consider introducing Version 2 without numbers so that students can have a chance to practice creating dialogue on the spot.

Extension

- Once students have mastered both versions, the teacher can switch up the operations, calling them out just as the scene begins.

Zip! Zap! Zop! (Math Version)

> **Improv Level:** Beginner
>
> **Grade Level:** 3rd grade and up
>
> **Time Needed:** 30 minutes
>
> **Materials:** None

This fun activity, used by many actors to build energy and sharpen focus before a performance, can be easily extended to make memorizing and drilling math facts a fun, social activity.

Directions

Version 1: These directions are for the generic version of game. Teach students this version first before introducing the math elements.

Everyone stands in a circle. The teacher begins by making eye contact with one student and claps her hands toward that student, saying, "Zip!" This student then chooses another student and proceeds as the teacher did, this time saying, "Zap!" The third student says, "Zop!," then "Zip!," and so on, with the three words repeating, always in the order zip!, zap!, zop! A student may choose anyone to zap! (or zip!, or zop!), except the person who has passed it to him, and he must say the words in the correct sequence. Further, once students have learned the rules, it should proceed on a regular beat.

Math Versions: Once students are comfortable with the generic version of the game, introduce these mathematical extensions.

- *Arithmetic:* Instead of *zip!, zap!,* and *zop!,* have students pass arithmetic equations. For example, the teacher might start out with seven. The next student might say, "times," a third could say, "six," a fourth would say, "equals," and the fifth would have to produce the answer. Then, another player starts a new equation.
- *Skip Counting:* Try counting by twos, threes, fives, or tens.
- *Memorizing:* Use this format for memorizing a formula or tool, such as the Order of Operations. Instead of passing around *zip!, zap!,* and *zop!,* have students pass around the elements of the formula: "parentheses," "exponents," "multiplication," "division," "addition," "subtraction."

Hint

- When students are excited about the game, it may be difficult to get them to focus after a mistake is made. Try indicating that the game is about to restart by patting your lap and saying, "Reaaaddddy."

Side Coaching

- "Keep it moving!"
- "Enunciate! Say the words as clearly as you can."

Chapter 6

Improv in the Content Areas

In the first chapter of this book we said that learning is more than just the acquisition of knowledge, it is an activity that people create together. While this might be easier to see in the case of learning to work in a group or even learning to read, we believe that it is also true of learning across the content areas. In this chapter, we provide improv activities that can be used to introduce children to the performance of learning in and about the two subjects, other than literacy and math, that are most common to elementary and middle school classrooms: social studies and science.

THE PERFORMANCE OF SCIENCE AND SOCIAL STUDIES

Academic subjects are a body of accumulated knowledge about a particular topic, but they also have a culture of their own—a language and a way of seeing the world. In order to be considered a historian, it is not enough to just know the facts about a particular period; one must also be able to think, talk, and write historically. In order to be a biologist, one must be able to use the language of cells and ecosystems with ease. Anyone who has ever asked a question of someone who is an expert in a subject is quickly aware of the specialized language and culture of different subject areas; that is why experts are often asked, "Could you say that again in plain English?"

Another way of thinking about this, and one that shouldn't surprise the readers of this book, is that these subject areas are performances that have been created over time and that continue to evolve. Real human beings, working together and separately, have created the fields of history, chemistry, art, anthropology, and so on—and the performances of what it means to be an expert in these areas. This is not to dismiss the specialized training and knowledge that are required to be a historian, a chemist, an artist, or an anthropologist. However, the information alone does not make someone an expert. Being able to speak the language and do the performance of these subjects is necessary to being able to acquire and create knowledge.

Improv activities provide a great opportunity for children to perform as historians, biologists, chemists, and anthropologists. In activities such as "Grab Bag," "Collective Tour Guide," and "Slide Show," children can perform as experts in these fields. For example, in "Grab Bag" children are encouraged to use scientific talk to describe a set of objects they have never seen before. Because children are freed from the constraints of being right or having to know the content, they are more able to play with the language of the profession. In "Three-Headed Expert" children might use their "Yes, and" skills to create a collective performance of a paleontologist being interviewed on the extinction of the dinosaurs. Since no one person is asked to answer the questions, the challenge is to create together the language an expert on dinosaurs might use.

Researchers have long argued that one of the values of preschool children's dramatic play is that it allows them to practice or play with adult roles and responsibilities. Children learn about the roles of firefighter, mommy, and chef by becoming those characters. However, as children get older and the subject matter becomes more abstract, they stop having opportunities to perform adult roles. The historian and the genetic engineer are not jobs that are a part of children's everyday experience. They don't walk down the street and meet historians at work, or watch TV and see genetic engineers. In addition, while high school students have teachers who are specialists in specific subject areas (history, biology, etc.), elementary school teachers rarely see themselves as historians, chemists, or anthropologists. This makes it difficult for teachers to model these professions, but improv can help to create an environment where teachers and children can perform these roles. Improv provides an opportunity to create these performances together—to play at what it means to be a historian, a chemist, or an anthropologist.

PERFORMING AHEAD OF YOURSELF

In addition to providing opportunities to perform as experts, improv also creates an environment where children can perform ahead of themselves as emerging learners of the content of science and social studies. To return to the paradox we discussed in Chapter 1, learning involves doing what you don't know how to do. Imagine how little babies would learn if they were only allowed to say and do the things they already knew something about. It may seem self-evident, but children need to be able to learn about science or social studies in an environment where they do not need to know anything about the subject.

On the other hand, the way science and social studies are typically taught in schools tends to be very information-driven, and the children who enjoy them and learn the most about them are often those who are already familiar with them through out-of-school experiences. In the last few years, researchers have confirmed that the achievement gap between poor and working-class children and their middle-class counterparts can, in part, be attributed to the experiences that children have outside school. Another way to put this is that middle-class children come to school with life experiences that provide a foundation on which school learning can occur. These children can access the social studies and science curricula because they have had life experiences that make them make sense.

So what does this have to do with improv? Improv can get all children involved in activities and discussions about social studies and science regardless of how well they are prepared, because it doesn't depend on prior knowledge. The structure of many improv games allows children to say or do things that are beyond what they could say or do under more traditional school conditions. It introduces children to the terminology of these fields in a supportive environment. For example, in creating an improvised scene that takes place on the moon, one child might begin walking in a funny way and the group could then use this offer to discover how they might move in a gravity-free environment. Each child does not need to worry if he or she knows anything about gravity—they just need to follow the game. In improv, children have an amazing capacity to contribute to the collective creation without getting stuck on what they do or do not know.

PERFORMING AS MEANING-MAKERS

While improv can energize any classroom, regardless of teaching philosophy, the kind of learning that happens with improv is in line with current learning theories that stress the importance of children constructing their knowledge. As one example, constructivist educators argue that children should not be just consumers of information; they need to have an opportunity to make meaning of what they are learning. In order to do this, children need to actively engage with discipline-specific knowledge in ways that allow them to think critically and become meaning-makers.

In improv there is no meaning other than what the participants create. While improvisers use material from the audience or from their lives, it is in the creation of the scene that this material comes to make any sense at all. When doing improv with the content of the curriculum, children can use what they have read in their textbooks as a starting-off point for their improvised scenes, but it is by creating something new with that material that children make meaning of what they have read.

Take for example, the improv activity "Correspondence," where the class improvises a series of letters between two historical figures (e.g., Desmond Tutu and F. W. de Klerk), and in the course of that activity they come to know these people in a way that is not possible from just reading about them in a book. Now, those letters should and would be informed by what the children have learned about Tutu and de Klerk, but by being allowed to play with what they have read, the children have an opportunity to make sense of history by putting themselves inside the story and making meaning of it as active, rather than passive, recipients of information.

Improv has the potential to introduce elementary and middle school children to some of the more sophisticated and up-to-date ideas about knowledge—ideas that are usually reserved for high school or beyond. In the last several decades there has been a shift in how experts understand what it means to know something in the social and even the physical and biological sciences. Even hard-core scientists have embraced the idea that what we know is rapidly changing, continuously created, and subjective. In the past, the job of the expert was to try to place oneself outside of whatever was being studied in order to gain an objective understanding of the phenomenon. However, scientists have come to realize not only that total objectivity is impossible, but that attempting it actually limits what one can learn. Subjectivity has come to be accepted as an unavoidable part of being human and can even be seen as a resource.

While this is how many experts in the field now work, it is not how children are taught. Young children learn about social studies and science as if these subjects were static bodies of knowledge that they should internalize. This contradiction makes it difficult for children as they grow older and are expected to become critical thinkers and creators of knowledge. When they arrive in high school and college they have had little experience with the fluidity and creativity involved in the subjects they are studying.

Improv is about creating rather than knowing, and it therefore provides children with an opportunity to develop a more flexible and creative relationship to ideas and theories. Improv includes creativity, risk-taking, and thinking outside the box, all of which support an understanding of social studies and science that is more in line with current practices in those fields. In the activities "What If?" and "Tableau," the class creates their own version of events or retells the official version from multiple perspectives. While it is obviously important that children learn the "facts" rather than myths or suppositions, it is equally important that they learn that "facts" have a history, they change, and they will continue to change, and that it is ordinary people like them who discover and create new knowledge.

IMPROVISING AND INFORMATION

We firmly believe that the most valuable learning occurs when children are making meaning; however, improv is also a very useful tool when students need to remember information. Memorization is clearly not the same thing as learning, yet it is a significant part of being a successful student. In addition to being useful in terms of accessing information for a test, being able to remember something is often helpful in being able to make creative use of the information.

Only a small percentage of people can hear a lecture or read a book and retain and make use of the information. Most people must have an active experience in order to remember what they have been taught and, more importantly, in order to make use of that information in other contexts. There are several ways that improv can be useful for remembering what has been taught. Some improv activities can serve as a mnemonic device. For example, children can throw the names of the continents around the circle as if they were a rubber ball in a variation of the "Sound Ball" activity. Or the class can compete for who can remember the most mammal names in the "One-Track Mind" activity. Finally, the excitement of performing as Rosa Parks being interviewed by a reporter about the Montgomery bus boycott in "Talk Show" is more likely to stick in a child's mind than reading a paragraph in a history book. In general, the active nature of improv helps children remember what they have learned and makes it more likely that they will be able to recall it on a test or in a future school or life situation.

While we have confidence that improv can help to transform teaching and learning in the content areas, we recognize that there are some risks and limits to its usefulness. Social studies and science in elementary schools usually follow a set curriculum; there are particular things that children are supposed to learn. In trying to fit those items into an improv format, it is possible to lose the emergent, non-truth-driven nature of improvisation. Improv might become one more place where children have to get it right and the children who are good at learning facts and skills become more successful than those who are not. If we fully maintain the integrity of the improv activity and accept all offers as valuable, do we run the risk of leaving children with misconceptions about the facts they will be assessed on?

There are ways to deal with these issues. Be clear when improv is being used with content knowledge that is going to be tested or that requires a right answer in order to do something else. Don't put too many parameters on the games—for example, an activity might involve creating a scene about what took place at the Tiananmen Square protests, and the class can decide that there are several important facts that must be included (e.g., who was there, what date it was), but the children should be free to be creative and add things spontaneously. If what you require is a direct rendition of what was said about the event in the textbook, then it is probably not an appropriate moment for an improvised scene. Finally, create playful ways of correcting that can include the rest of the class. For example, there can be a team of children who are comparing the events in the improv scene to the facts in the textbook and listing them on the board or in a Venn diagram. We encourage you to be creative about how you include these activities in your teaching—find ways to adapt the games to your particular needs, but make sure not to take the creativity out of them.

Learning involves building relationships—relationships to our fellow learners, but also to the subject matter itself. Improv can provide a way to bring laughter, creativity, and spontaneity to children's relationships with the content of the curriculum and can help them to make it their own. If teachers recognize that they are helping children form their first relationships to these subjects, then they can help children to create and develop a relationship that can serve them well now and in the future.

SETUP OF THE CHAPTER

In improv there are a group of activities that are commonly referred to as "handles." Handles are frameworks that can be used with any suggestion. For example, a "Talk Show" handle may have a similar format every time, with a host interviewing a famous guest, but who the guest is and therefore the content of the interview will always be different. Handles are an ideal ways to include content area knowledge because they are flexible and can be used with any topic, yet they give a structure within which to explore the content in creative ways.

The activities in this chapter are divided into three sections. The first section is devoted to activities, most of which are improv handles, that can be adapted for either science or social studies. The second section focuses on activities where children can learn social studies content and explore the performances of social scientists. In the final section, the activities are focused on the life, physical, and environmental sciences and the performances of the scientist.

General Content Area Activities

The activities in this section can be used with almost any topic. They are particularly good for creating an environment where children can perform ahead of themselves. The design of these games provides a framework that allows students to take risks and collectively make discoveries about a topic.

We Are All . . .

Improv Level: Beginner

Grade Level: Kindergarten through 3rd grade

Time Needed: 10 minutes

Materials: None

Fans of "Follow the Leader" will find this exercise familiar. In addition to creating an environment where all offers are accepted, students physically explore topics they are studying in social studies and science.

Directions

Everyone walks around the room, changing directions and working to use the entire space. After a few minutes the teacher calls out, "We are all . . ." and then suggests something that the class can act out from a given category, such as jobs, animals, or fictional characters. The students then continue walking around while they all perform as giraffes or firefighters.

Hint

- Encourage students to invent their own ideas for how to act out their character. Highlight unique or creative examples.

Side Coaching

- "How does your character move? Where is your character going?"

Extensions

- Once students are comfortable with the routine, change the rules so that instead of the teacher calling out suggestions, anyone can make a suggestion after a few moments. Remind the students to allow time for each idea to be acted out and that only one suggestion can be done at a time.

Sentence Shuffle

Improv Level: Beginner

Grade Level: 2nd grade and up

Time Needed: 20 minutes

Materials: At least 1 index card and 1 pencil for each student

This simple exercise allows students to go beyond sharing what they know about a topic to making connections between ideas. With younger children, the idea of "staying on topic" can be explored through successful and unsuccessful performances of building on a fellow student's idea.

Directions

Every student is given an index card and instructed to write one sentence about a topic the class has been studying. The cards are then collected, shuffled, and redistributed, one card to each student. The students take turns reading the sentence on their new card and then adding a second sentence, beginning with the words "Yes, and." For example, when studying a unit on weather, the first student might write, "Water freezes at 32 degrees Fahrenheit." The student reading the card would add, "Yes, and this is the temperature where rain turns to snow."

Side Coaching

- "What's the very next thing you would expect to read or hear about that topic?"

Extension

- Have students write the second sentence on the card. Reshuffle and distribute the cards again, adding a third or even a fourth line. Extend the exercise into a nonfiction writing activity where students collectively write essays about a given topic.

Fish Bowl

Improv Level: Advanced

Grade Level: 3rd grade and up

Time Needed: 20 minutes

Materials: "Fish bowl" (basket or box); small slips of paper and pencils

Sometimes the most interesting things happen when something completely out of context is said. This activity is an example of those moments and is designed to allow students to access and explore the language of a discipline without the need for mastery or prior knowledge. The challenge of incorporating lines from a text into ordinary dialogue will help your students find and create connections to material that may be unfamiliar. Because the phrases they must integrate into their scene will likely have nothing to do with its premise, they can embrace the absurdity and carry on.

Directions

The class prepares slips of paper with brief phrases taken directly from a textbook or some other written material (e.g., "The Senate is made up of two elected officials from every state of the union"). Two or three students are chosen to play the scene. The class suggests a setting and roles for each performer, for example, a mother and father with their child at the zoo. The performers begin the scene and after a few moments, one at a time, they are offered the fish bowl, at which point they must randomly select a slip of paper and read it as though it makes perfect sense for their character to say that line at just that moment. Here is a quick example of what these scenes might look like:

> *Performer 1:* Mommy, that bear is so cute.
> *Performer 2:* He's cute, but I wouldn't want to get too close.
> *Performer 3* (taking a slip of paper out of the bowl): The Senate is made up of two elected officials from every state in the union— and I wouldn't want to get too close to them, either.
> *Performer 1:* Dad, has a bear ever been elected to the Senate?

The scene continues until all the slips of paper have been used or the director feels it's been long enough and calls, "Curtain."

Hint

- It is the job of everyone in the scene to make each line fit. They must accept the (likely) absurd statement and build on it to further the scene.

Side Coaching

- "Stay in character. Make it seem as though the line was exactly what you wanted to say/hear."

Extension

- Have students pick only two phrases from the bowl. They must begin the scene with the first and end it with the second.

One-Track Mind

Improv Level: Advanced

Grade Level: 3rd grade and up

Time Needed: 20 minutes

Materials: None

Do you have students who love to dominate a conversation? Or only like to talk about one thing? "One-Track Mind" is premised on the idea of making every conversation about that one topic you love to talk about, but which might not be of interest to those around you. Knowing a lot (or at least performing like you know a lot) and being fascinated by the subject is part of the game, thus removing the stigma of seeming like a geek or monopolizing the conversation.

Directions

The game begins with two students talking together in front of the class or with the whole class divided into pairs of students. One character, the Knower, chooses or is assigned a category, for example trains. The pair is also given a setting where two people might have a conversation, such as the playground. As the scene begins, the two start having an ordinary conversation. The job of the Knower is to make everything that comes up in the conversation be about that one topic. For example, if the category is trains, the Knower might respond to a statement about a new baby brother by mentioning that "Babies get to ride free on most trains."

Hint

- The student who is not the Knower is responsible for looking out for the progression of the scene, taking extra care to see that offers are accepted and built on.
- It's okay, and even encouraged, for the Knower to make things up in order to keep the conversation going.

Side Coaching

- To the Knower: "Try to get her to talk about trains."
- To the student who is not the Knower: "Keep the conversation moving. Accept the offer and keep going."

Extension

- More advanced students may play a version of the game where instead of saying "that reminds me of . . ." the Knower tries to insert as many references to their topic as possible (in pun-like fashion). For example, someone fascinated with mammals would try to work the names of as many mammals as possible into the conversation: "We had a whale of a good time at that party, but Alex ate like a pig, so we ran out of food."

Persuasion

Improv Level: Intermediate

Grade Level: 2nd grade and up

Time Needed: 20 minutes

Materials: None

Persuasion is a powerful form of discourse involving not just persuasive words but persuasive volume, tone, and gesture. Removing a piece of text from its context and using the words in an absurd manner allows students to play and create with content area language in a new way.

Directions

Two students volunteer to stand in front of the group. One is the Persuader and the other the Persuaded. Each student is given a short sentence extracted from a text they have been reading or will be reading for an upcoming unit (e.g., "An environment is made up of everything that surrounds an organism, including the air, water, soil, and even other organisms"). Taking suggestions from the group, the Persuader must convince the Persuaded to do something, such as loan him or her a pencil, using only the line they have been given from the text. The Persuaded refuses, using only his or her line, until eventually he or she gives in.

Hint

- If students struggle after a few attempts, have two students play the scene using any words they choose. While they do this, instruct other students to take note of the tone of voice and any gestures or mannerisms the Persuader and Persuaded employ during the scene. Then try the scene again in the original way.

Side Coaching

- "Use your body to convince him/her."
- "Show her you mean 'no!'"

Extensions

- Instead of persuading, students can argue, sing a popular tune, or teach a lesson using lines of dialogue.
- Advanced students can act out an entire scene using a textbook as their script, where each time they speak they read the next line from the text.

Hot Seat (Content Area Version)

Improv Level: Intermediate

Grade Level: 2nd grade and up

Time Needed: 20 minutes

Materials: None

Sometimes the power of improv is that the absurdity of the activity helps students get beyond the constraints of trying to be right and encourages them to talk without knowing what they are talking about. This exercise will help your class perform under pressure, and will allow them to say more than they think they know.

Directions

Three students sit in a row in front of the class. The student in the middle is in the Hot Seat. The student to the left of him begins to engage him in a conversation about a topic related to a social studies or science curriculum. After about 30 seconds, the student on the right begins a conversation with the student in the Hot Seat about an entirely new social studies or science topic. The job of the student in the Hot Seat is to listen to and participate in both conversations at one time.

Hint

• Students will need to learn to listen in a new way in order to be successful in the Hot Seat. This game is not about saying all the right things, it's about taking the risk to respond.

Side Coaching

• To the students in the side chairs: "Don't try to trick the player in the Hot Seat. Take care of the conversation. Everything he/she says is an offer. Build with it to keep the conversation going."

Collective Tour Guide

Improv Level: Intermediate

Grade Level: 3rd grade and up

Time Needed: 30 minutes

Materials: A small sign on a stick displaying the slogan of the class's tour company (i.e., "Ms. Shapiro's Super Tours")

A really good tour guide—someone who can tell you things about a place that don't appear in the guidebooks—can make any trip interesting. This activity puts your students in that role as they collectively take a visitor on a tour of a place or an environment, thus introducing students to the world beyond their immediate experience. They can "travel" to environments they may not easily be able to visualize or visit, such as a plant cell, ancient Rome, or the surface of Mars.

Directions

Between 5 and 10 students are chosen to sit together on one side of the class and function as the Collective Tour Guide. Their task is to give a tour of a location (the rain forest, the settlement at Jamestown, the surface of Mars) to the rest of the class. The students giving the tour take turns pointing out interesting features or facts about the location they are representing. Whoever has the tour sign is the speaker, and the sign is passed around to give everyone an opportunity to speak. The rest of the class, acting collectively as the Tourist, should periodically ask questions about the location.

Hints

- If students are reluctant to speak, have them give the tour one sentence at a time, with each student saying one sentence and then passing the sign to his or her neighbor.
- If the students in the Collective Tour Guide do not seem to be following one another, have them give the tour using "Yes, and."

Side Coaching

- "Remember, you're an expert on this place. Even if you're unsure about what you're saying, talk as though you're confident in everything you're saying."

Three-Headed Expert

Improv Level: Intermediate

Grade Level: 2nd grade and up

Time Needed: 20 minutes

Materials: None

As we discussed in this chapter's introduction, performing as an expert allows children insight into the fields they are studying and helps to build connections to the source of knowledge discovery and creation. By performing as the expert, even when they know very little about a subject matter, students can play with the language of expertness and develop skills at discourse and presentation.

Directions

Three members of the class are invited to perform as a single Three-Headed Expert. They do not need to have advanced knowledge about the field being discussed; what is important is that the scene be performed as though they do. These three students stand very close together and perform as one person. Another member of the class is chosen to be the Interviewer. The Interviewer's performance is just as important as the Expert's—the Interviewer can develop her own character or emulate a famous interviewer (e.g., Oprah Winfrey). The Interviewer should be curious about both the subject matter and the Expert, and should support everything the Expert says. The scene proceeds with a brief interview where the Expert answers questions using a "Yes, and" format. Each of the heads says one sentence and then the next head says, "Yes, and" and adds the next sentence of the answer. The Three-Headed Expert performs as confident and knowledgeable even if neither is the case. The Interviewer may also invite questions from the class/audience.

Hint

- Share brief samples of television interviews for the class to imitate. Highlight characteristics of a confident expert performance. Encourage students to add an arrogant edge to their Experts.

Side Coaching

- "Make something up. Convince us that you know what you're talking about, even if you don't."

Extension

- Perform the exercise as above, but with each of the "heads" only saying one word at a time.

We Can Sell Anything

Improv Level: Beginner

Grade Level: 3rd grade and up

Time Needed: 30 minutes or more, depending on group size

Materials: Slips of paper with the names of tools, organisms, or concepts students are studying

Advertising professionals are well paid for their keen skill at narrowing in on what is powerful, meaningful, and desirable about the product they are trying to sell. In this activity students do the impossible by very quickly putting together a sales pitch about a concept or organism they have been studying.

Directions

Students are broken up into groups of four. One group comes up to the front of the room. The group is given one slip of paper with the name of what they are trying to sell. Examples could include a microscope, democracy, Hawaii, or a squid. They have 5 minutes to complete the following tasks:

1. Talk about the importance of this product, tool, organism, or concept.
2. Tell the audience why they should buy it.
3. Pick a celebrity spokesperson for the product.
4. Make up a jingle or a poem that can help sell this product.
5. Create and perform a quick commercial for this product that includes all of these elements.

Hint

- Remind students that this is really a version of "Yes, and"—if they accept and use everyone's offers, they will succeed in creating a commercial.

Side Coaching

- "Remember that this is a version of 'Yes, and'—accept your partner's offers."
- "What's the best thing about your product?"
- "Who are you trying to sell it to? Why would they like it?"

Extension

- If the exercise is a hit, consider building a regular "Home Shopping Channel"–type format where products are presented one after another with a host introducing inventors and company presidents who pitch their products one after another.

Social Studies Activities

The activities in this section allow children to play with the concepts of time and space and the relationships between people and events, and to experience the content of history, government, civics, and economics firsthand. They provide a vehicle for helping children become more worldly, by putting them into the stories rather than seeing themselves as consumers of information. They give children the sense of themselves as history-makers. Finally, these activities provide children with an opportunity to use their subjective experiences to become conversant in the most subjective subject of all—the study of human life.

I Love My Neighbor

Improv Level: Beginner

Grade Level: Kindergarten through 3rd grade

Time Needed: 10 minutes

Materials: None

This fun activity will dovetail nicely with early elementary school curricula exploring classroom communities. As students are challenged to think of various descriptive categories, they can further their understanding of what makes individuals alike and different. Students will be surprised to learn what they have in common that is not readily apparent.

Directions

The class stands in a circle except for one student, who stands in the middle. That student begins by saying, "I love my neighbor who . . . ," naming a characteristic that some students in the class might have, for example, "I love my neighbor who is wearing blue shoes" or "I love my neighbor who has a sister." Each student with that characteristic must quickly switch places with another student elsewhere in the circle who has that characteristic in common. While they are racing to trade places, the student in the middle must attempt to take one of the empty spots. The student who is unable to find a spot is now in the middle and calls out a new characteristic. If a characteristic is called out that no one has, the same student remains in the middle and tries again.

Hint

- Be aware of the potential for collisions in the middle of the circle. Remind students that safety is a greater priority than getting to an empty spot.

Side Coaching

- "Think of a characteristic that isn't physical (that you can't see)."

Occupation

Improv Level: Intermediate

Grade Level: Kindergarten through 3rd grade

Time Needed: 20 minutes

Materials: None

Occupations are a common and important component of early childhood and elementary social studies curricula. This activity allows students to explore those roles while challenging their skill at working together to improvise quickly and collaboratively.

Directions

Two teams of about five students are selected, and each team retires to a corner of the room where they cannot be heard by the other team. They are given 3 minutes to select an occupation (police officer, train conductor) and to come up with a short, silent performance that represents that occupation. They then come to the stage and create their performance without using the name of the job. Students can each perform a separate representation of that profession (for example, all five students listening to an imaginary patient's heart), or they can build a unified scene (a doctor and his team performing an operation on a patient). After each team has mimed their occupation, the other team is given one guess. If they are not correct, they may ask a question that the other team can perform, such as, "What kind of building do you work in?" This continues until the occupation is guessed.

Hint

- It may be difficult for younger students to guess the occupation. Consider having students select from a list of specific professions they have been studying.

Side Coaching

- While each group is planning: "What is something your character does that everyone is familiar with?"

Extension

- This activity can be used with almost any category of things— ecosystems, government institutions, seasons.

Time Warp

Improv Level: Intermediate

Grade Level: 3rd grade and up

Time Needed: 20 minutes

Materials: None

Stepping into history gets a unique twist as students are given the opportunity to make and see clear connections between their lives and the lives of young people during a time period they are studying.

Directions

Two or three students stand in front of the class. They choose an ordinary scene from their own daily lives (walking to school, playing soccer). Next, they must replay the same scene as though they were in a historic time period they have been studying as a class, substituting activities, objects, and conversation that would have been common during that time period.

Hints

- Students may need help coming up with ideas that correlate between contemporary activities and historic ones.
- Involve the class in brainstorming suggestions as the performers consider how to create their historical scene.

Side Coaching

- "What would they be making/doing?"
- "How did people travel back then?"
- "What current events might they have been discussing?"

What If? (History Version)

Improv Level: Advanced

Grade Level: 3rd grade and up

Time Needed: 30 minutes

Materials: None

The study of history is enormously truth-driven. Traditionally, students are presented with a set of facts about what happened and asked to reproduce those facts on an exam. While it is important to know and understand "what really happened," it is also fun for students to have an opportunity to play with what history is, to put themselves in it, and to explore the infinite ways it could unfold. Developing this relationship with specific subject matter and the discipline of history itself will help students become more engaged and sophisticated learners.

Directions

A small group of students is invited to the front of the stage and carefully discusses with the class the circumstances of an important historical scene, such as the signing of the Declaration of Independence. The teacher assigns roles and the students re-create the scene as accurately as possible. After a few minutes the teacher freezes the action and asks for a suggestion from the audience of something that could happen instead of what they just saw (the pen doesn't work, John Hancock gets in a fight with Benjamin Franklin about who gets to sign first). The action continues, incorporating this new suggestion, until a few minutes later when the action is frozen again and a new prompt is solicited.

Hints

- When first introducing this activity, it may be necessary for the teacher to supply the prompts to help students understand what kinds of suggestions are most helpful.
- Try to avoid inserting a "better" version of history by suggesting how you wish the scene might have turned out. The more absurd the suggestion, the better.

Side Coaching

- "Stay in character."
- "How would your character react to this situation?"

Correspondence

Improv Level: Intermediate

Grade Level: 3rd grade and up

Time Needed: 25 minutes

Materials: None

Until very recently, letter-writing was an important mode of communication, and it is a significant source of material for historians. Letters uncover otherwise unspoken elements of a period of history and present historical figures in a human light often obscured in other, more public documents. By collectively improvising letters, students can add their own ideas and pose questions about what these figures may have been thinking.

Directions

The class is separated into two groups, sitting in two semicircles facing each other. Each group is assigned the role of an anonymous person from a historical period (for example, a stone carver and a peasant farmer in medieval Europe) or a pair of famous people who knew one another (Sacagawea and Meriwether Lewis). One group goes first, using the format of "Yes, and" to write a letter to the other character, with the first sentence being "Dear so-and-so" and the final sentence, "Sincerely, so-and-so." After the first group finishes their "letter," the other group "writes" a reply following the same format.

Hint

- Discuss or read examples of letters to teach or remind students of the conventions of letter writing. Encourage students to ask questions of and respond to the other character.

Side Coaching

- "Remember to respond to the other group."
- "What do you think Sacagawea would want Lewis to know about her life?"
- "What did you (your character) do for fun last weekend?"

Extension

- Have students write collective letters on a clipboard in their respective groups, where everyone takes turns adding a sentence to the letter, and then "send it" to the other group.

Rant or Rave

Improv Level: Intermediate

Grade Level: 1st grade and up

Time Needed: 20 minutes

Materials: Brightly colored "Rant" and "Rave" signs

Most of us have had the experience of listening to someone go on and on about how amazing or terrible something is. The improvised performance of ranting and raving gives students an opportunity to see these activities as performances and allows them to play the role of impassioned spokesperson, which in turn adds depth to their understanding of the subject matter. Having to rant or rave about a topic encourages students to go beyond what they think they know about a subject and creatively build on that knowledge.

Directions

Two performers are chosen and are given a topic related to something the class has been studying. One of them is arbitrarily assigned the role of the Ranter and the other that of the Raver. The Ranter performs as if he is adamant about his disdain for that topic or position and presents a fierce argument extolling its weaknesses and negative qualities. The Raver, however, is incredibly enthusiastic about the subject matter and cannot stop talking about how wonderful it is. Both performers stand facing the audience and simultaneously begin their rants and raves. They are not responding to one another and do not need to be able to hear what the other is saying. The teacher or a director may choose to use hand signals to suggest that one of the performers speak more quietly or more loudly for a few moments to highlight their words, much like an orchestra conductor.

Hints

- Discuss and practice ranting and raving. Consider having students first perform the exercise using examples from their own lives about which they are either enthusiastically pro or con.
- Remind students that they are not debating or competing. Each performer is presenting a separate monologue.

Side Coaching

- "Keep talking. Don't worry about whether or not we can understand you."
- "Make your case. You really believe in this!"

Extension

- Have choruses of Ranters and Ravers who are all ranting and raving about different topics.

Tableau

Improv Level: Intermediate
Grade Level: 2nd grade and up
Time Needed: 25 minutes
Materials: None

Social studies books are filled with famous pictures. These paintings and photographs tell us what historical figures looked like and show us a perspective on the world they lived in. Many of these scenes, such as George Washington's crossing of the Delaware, have become images that shape our understanding of the events more than anything that has been written about them. In this activity, students step into these famous pictures and then bring them to life, uncovering what these distant figures might have been thinking or saying to one another.

Directions

The class selects a famous picture to re-create. One student is chosen as the Painter (or Photographer), whose job it is to "sculpt" students into a frozen recreation of a picture in their textbook. As many students are used as there are people in the scene, and others can perform as animals or important inanimate objects. The Painter should take as much time as he or she needs to make the image as realistic as possible. Once the Painter is satisfied, the teacher points to each student in the scene one at a time, having them share with the class what they, as their famous character, were thinking in that moment.

Hints

- Encourage students to get into character while they are being posed. This will give them time to think about what might have been on the mind of their character at that moment.
- Remind students that even famous people could have been thinking about ordinary things, such as having an itch or wondering what they will eat for supper. If these things seem fitting, they can be included among more significant musings.

Side Coaching

- "What was important to your character at that moment?"
- "What were you feeling? Were you scared? Excited?"

Extension

- Re-create the image as above. Instead of pointing to each character, unfreeze the performers by saying, "Action." Once unfrozen, the cast begins a scene about what happened right after the image from the textbook was captured.

Party Game

Improv Level: Advanced

Grade Level: 3rd grade and up

Time Needed: 25 minutes

Materials: None

Children love parties. Well, what would happen if the guests were characters from the social studies curriculum (e.g., Cleopatra, a postal worker, or a Chinese emperor)? In this exercise students perform as famous characters or familiar professionals brought together for a party. Something can be discovered about these figures by seeing how they interact with others in this unusual or absurd context.

Directions

Four students are selected to perform this activity for the whole class. One student serves as the Host of the party. She leaves the room for a few minutes while the class assigns each of the other three performers with an identity. They can be professionals, such as firefighters or geologists, or famous figures, such as Martin Luther King Jr. or Hillary Clinton. When the Host returns, she begins the scene by setting out imaginary plates of food and arranging imaginary decorations while the Guests step off stage. One at a time, each Guest rings an imaginary doorbell and arrives at the party, performing just as his character might. The Host can take his coat, offer something to eat, exchange greetings, and begin a conversation. In the course of the conversation the Guest gives hints about his identity without saying the name, and the Host asks questions that will allow him to figure out the identity of the Guest. This continues until the Host is able to guess the identity of the Guest. Guessing should also be done within the reality of the scene, for example, by saying, "It's so great to have such a famous civil rights figure in my home, Dr. King." As soon as one Guest's identity is guessed, a second Guest rings the doorbell and the first Guest moves offstage. This continues until all three Guests have been identified.

Hints

- Work with the Host to help her ask questions, or suggest topics to bring up with the Guests that will be helpful in discovering who they are.
- Remind the Guests that the objective is not to fool the Host. They are to perform their part as realistically as they can and answer questions fully, as would be consistent with their characters.

Side Coaching

- To the Host: "Ask about how his/her day was."
- To the Guest: "How would your character answer that question?"

Extension

- Once students build their skill at asking revealing questions, try a version of the game where the second Guest arrives only a minute after the first, whether the Host has guessed his or her identity or not. Eventually all three Guests are onstage interacting while the Host attempts to guess who they are.

History Bus

Improv Level: Intermediate

Grade Level: 3rd grade and up

Time Needed: 25 minutes

Materials: None

Have you ever wondered what Gandhi, Julius Caesar, and Betsy Ross might say to one another? This exercise provides the class with the opportunity to explore just these kinds of questions, and in doing so, get to know historical figures in a new way.

Directions

Chairs are arranged in the front of the classroom to represent seats on a school bus. A performer is selected to act as the Bus Driver, and several other performers are chosen to play famous historical figures. The Bus Driver sits in his or her seat and "picks up" each of the other performers one at a time, who enter the bus in character and begin a conversation with the other characters as they arrive.

Hint

- Remind students to think about what their character might do on a school bus.

Side Coaching

- "Who would you sit with?"
- "What would you talk about?"
- "Are you comfortable on the bus?"
- "Who are you friendly/unfriendly with?"

Visitor from the Past

Improv Level: Intermediate

Grade Level: 2nd grade and up

Time Needed: 20 minutes

Materials: None

This exercise provides another way to make the past come alive. This time, however, rather than transporting students into the past, the exercise brings the past to them. Students can explore similarities and differences and gain perspective on how their worlds and their language have changed over time.

Directions

Two volunteers are invited to perform for the class. One student performs as the Visitor from the past. The person has arrived in the classroom after being magically transported into the present day. The students are assigned a modern object (a cell phone, a film projector), and the second student must describe that object, including its function, to the Visitor, using only words and ideas that he or she would understand. The job of the Visitor is to express confusion or ask clarifying questions when something is referenced that he or she would not understand given his or her historical perspective.

Hints

- Have the teacher play the Visitor the first few times.
- Coach students through the performances to ensure that the Visitor is adequately insisting that the modern performer find ways of making their descriptions sensible.

Side Coaching

- To the Visitor: "Would your character know what that is? Insist that your partner be specific."

Extension

- Once students have seen a few performances, have them break into groups of two and try various objects on their own. Invite students to return to a circle or the desks and discuss what they discovered.

Talk Show

Improv Level: Intermediate

Grade Level: 3rd grade and up

Time Needed: 30 minutes

Materials: 2 chairs, chalkboard and chalk or chart paper and markers

The talk show format is familiar to anyone who watches TV, even children. These shows are filled with drama that can add excitement and interest to a social studies unit. "Talk Show" can be used at the beginning of a unit to assess the class's level of familiarity with a particular character or topic, or to allow students to explore the role of a particular person in shaping a historical moment. At the end of a unit, "Talk Show" can be a fun way to assess what has been learned. Consider making "Talk Show" a recurring activity, allowing students to develop the character of the host, the announcer, and other players.

Directions

Chairs are arranged theater-style, in rows facing a stage (or children can sit at their desks and the front of the room can serve as the stage). The stage contains two chairs, facing one another as for a television talk show. This show features a Guest from a moment in history or an important figure from the present time. The show begins with an Announcer introducing the show, including the day's Guest and the Host, both of whom enter to applause from the Audience, played by the other members of the class. The Audience performs as though they were present for the taping of a real talk show—cheering, laughing, and even booing. Additional students can perform as camera operators or producers to add to the realism. The Host welcomes the Guest and asks a series of questions about his or her life, the circumstances of a particular event, or his or her opinion on significant issues. The Host may also choose to accept questions from the Audience. The game concludes with the Host thanking the Guest and telling the viewers what will happen on next week's show.

Hints

- Ask the class to brainstorm what they know about a character beforehand. Position this information so that it can be seen by the Guest to provide help when a response requires information he or she might not quickly recall.
- If the Guest is having a difficult time answering questions, use a tag-team format where someone from the Audience can trade places with the Guest and answer a tough question for him or her.

Side Coaching

- To the Host: "This is your show. Don't be afraid to ask hard questions."
- To the Guest: "Stay in character."
- To the Guest: "Do your best to answer the question, but remember you can always say, 'No comment.'"
- To the Audience: "You will be seen on TV. Perform as an audience."

Extension

- Invite two characters to perform as Guests on the show to discuss historic rivalries or significant collaborations (e.g, Gandhi and a British soldier, Thomas Jefferson and James Madison).

Helping Hands

Improv Level: Intermediate

Grade Level: 3rd grade and up

Time Needed: 20 minutes

Materials: None

Most of us don't realize how much information is communicated through hand gestures. By physically separating the speaker and the person responsible for making hand gestures, the role of gestures in communication is highlighted.

Directions

Four students stand at the front of the class in two pairs. One student in each pair places his hands behind his back, removing them from view of the audience. The other student in the pair stands behind her partner and slips her arms through her partner's arms and positions her hands so as to replace those of her partner. Each pair is assigned the role of an expert with opposing views on an important matter—for example, serving junk food in the cafeteria or searching people's backpacks on buses. The students then commence a debate, with the person in front providing the words and the person in back the accompanying hand movements.

Hints

- Consider adding props to heighten the drama and allow students to exaggerate the importance of the hands.
- Encourage students to see everything as an offer in this activity; the person speaking is making verbal offers that the "hands" can use, and the "hands" are making physical offers that the "voice" can use.

Side Coaching

- "Speak with your hands."
- "Accept all offers."

Science Activities

The activities in this section are for use in supporting children to perform as scientists and to assist learning in the areas of the physical, biological, and environmental sciences. Many of the activities involve playing with and exploring the core scientific concepts of change, interconnection, and environment. Other activities give children a chance to perform as scientists and to experience science as an activity that actual people do all the time and that is as much about not knowing as it is about being smart.

Three Changes

Improv Level: Beginner

Grade Level: All

Time Needed: 15 minutes

Materials: None

The study of change is a key topic in the elementary school science curriculum. In improvisation, as in science, small changes often make a big difference. This activity makes those changes explicit. And because students have to attend to detail, it also teaches critical observation skills.

Directions

The class breaks up into pairs and forms two parallel lines facing one another. One line is designated the A's and the other is the B's. The A's are instructed to look very carefully at their partners. The B's then move out of sight of the A's and make three subtle but noticeable changes to their appearances (e.g., removing their glasses, putting their hair behind their ears, unbuttoning their shirts). When they return, the A's attempt to figure out what changes were made by the B's. The A's then take their turn making changes and having the B's figure them out.

Hint

- Remind the students that the objective is not to trick their partners. Changes that are completely indistinguishable defeat the purpose of the activity.

Side Coaching

- "Examine your partner as though you are a scientist."

Ecosystem

Improv Level: Beginner

Grade Level: All

Time Needed: 20 minutes

Materials: None

This game, which is a content-specific "Make a Machine," gives students the opportunity to create an environment where each element is connected to another, thus helping them to see the relationships between the various elements that make up an ecosystem.

Directions

This game can be done either as a whole class or with the class split into two groups, with one group performing for the other. The class stands in a semicircle and the teacher selects an environment, such as a rain forest. Students are told that they are going to create an ecosystem. The first student steps onto the stage and begins miming a repetitive action and, if appropriate, repeating a noise representing some organism or feature of the environment (e.g., a toucan). There can be no speaking of actual words, unless a human being is in the ecosystem. Some examples could include a palm tree, a monkey eating fruit, or the ocean. After one person enters the scene, another follows with something that fits into the environment and is connected to what is already happening in the scene (e.g., the wind blowing the palm tree, the rock the monkey is sitting on, or a whale in the ocean). This continues until everyone has joined the scene.

Hint

- Encourage students not to try to think of something clever ahead of time.

Side Coaching

- "Look at the scene. What's missing?"
- "How does your element interact with the other parts of the ecosystem?"

Extensions

- Once students are familiar with the idea, they can attempt a version of the scene where everyone moves into the middle at once instead of one at a time.
- Remove or make a change to one organism in the ecosystem and see the effect on the total system. For example, "What happens if the waterfall stopped flowing?"
- This activity could also be used for social studies: Create a scene of a firehouse where everyone comes in as one component of that environment (e.g., a firefighter, a hose, a dog).

Boundaries

Improv Level: Intermediate

Grade Level: All

Time Needed: 20 minutes

Materials: Masking tape to mark off quadrants on the floor

Ever wonder what it would be like to walk on the moon, trek across a desert, or swim in the deepest part of the ocean? This is a classic improvisation exercise designed to help performers develop skills at creating and responding to an imaginary environment, which will give your students an opportunity to explore how the physical environment might affect them.

Directions

The classroom or other large space is divided into four quadrants, representing four different environments, geographic locations, or climates (e.g., desert, rain forest, tundra, and prairie). The students move slowly and silently around the classroom, changing their actions to match the characteristics of the quadrant they are in.

Hint

- Before adding all four quadrants, have students practice moving around as though the whole classroom had just one characteristic. As they do this, highlight creative examples of physical responses to the various environments.

Side Coaching

- "What's the temperature like?"
- "Is it easy to walk, or do you need to crawl?"
- "What do you notice? Show us what you're seeing."

Extension

- With older students, an unrelated scene (for example, a father and son having a fight) can be improvised on a performance space with four quadrants representing different environments or even emotions. The performers are given a relationship and begin their scene. When the action of the scene moves them from one quadrant to another, they incorporate that into their movement and dialogue.

Rain Noises

Improv Level: Beginner

Grade Level: All

Time Needed: 15 minutes

Materials: None

Imagine your students' delight when they collectively re-create the distinctive sounds of a summer rainstorm: the stirring wind, the first wet drops, the raucous downpour, and the eventual, gradual surcease. This activity provides a great opportunity to examine each of these elements as part of an exploration of weather. Once mastered, a class may choose to add elements, such as lightning, or create different kinds of storms.

Directions

The class stands in a large circle facing the teacher in the middle. The teacher begins by introducing, one at a time, each of the elements that will make up the class's rainstorm. The teacher makes the motion and has students repeat it. The first is the wind, made by placing the hands together, palm to palm, and rubbing swiftly back and forth. The second is the first few drops of rain, made either by snapping or clicking fingernails. The third is heavier rain, made by patting one's thighs with the flat palm of the hands. Once the class has practiced each element, the class is instructed on how the storm will be built. The teacher begins by facing one student and making the first motion, the wind. Only that student makes the wind noise. The teacher then moves clockwise around the circle to the next student, making the same wind noise. Everyone is to continue making the same noise until the teacher gets to him or her again with a new noise. The teacher continues around the circle with the same noise until she gets to the first student, at which point she makes the second noise, the raindrops. Students only change noises when the teacher faces them with a new noise, and otherwise they continue with the previous noise. The third element, heavy rain, is added. Next, the storm begins to subside, with the fourth element being a return to raindrops, then the fifth, wind, and finally the storm gradually stops.

Hints

- Students will likely need reminders to change their movements only when the teacher indicates that it is time.
- Before playing the game, have students close their eyes and listen to a new sound. Highlight the difference between the sound one person can make and what the class can make together.

Side Coaching

- "Wait until I get to you."

Extensions

- Have students invent new noises to add elements to the rainstorm, such as thunder. Create different sounds for a hurricane or a hailstorm.
- Rather than having the teacher walk around the circle, have the students turn and pass the sound to the next student.

Heartbeat

Improv Level: Beginner

Grade Level: All

Time Needed: 10 minutes

Materials: None

Lub-dub, Lub-dub, Lub-dub. . . . *Our heartbeat is a constant rhythm in our lives. This activity, which is a wonderful ensemble-building game, also gives students a way to learn about their pulse and how it relates to their physical activity.*

Directions

Everyone sits in a circle. The students are taught how to find their heartbeat, either by placing a hand on their heart or by checking their pulse on their neck or wrist. After feeling their heartbeat for a minute, have students begin clapping to the rhythm they feel. Encourage them to keep their rhythm going even if his or her neighbor has a different rhythm. Next, the class runs around the gym or the playground, or runs in place in their classroom for a few minutes. They then quickly return to the circle and again check their pulse and begin clapping to the new rhythm.

Hint

- Try to hear the rhythm in your head before you take your hand away from your pulse.

Side Coaching

- "Listen to the *group's* heartbeat."

Extension

- Have the students count the number of beats in one minute. Create a chart of the class's pulse at various times of day or following various levels of exercise, ranging from naptime to immediately following gym class.

I Am a Tree

Improv Level: Beginner

Grade Level: All

Time Needed: 15 minutes

Materials: None

This wonderfully organic and simple game helps students to see the relationships between and among various parts of a system. This game is easy to teach and provides ample opportunity for students to develop their understanding of relationships.

Directions

The class stands in a circle. One person is chosen to go first and enters the circle, strikes up a pose of any common object or organism that can be found in the world, and says, "I am . . . " and then the name of the object. For example, a performer may enter the circle, stand up straight with arms extended, and declare loudly, "I am a tree!" At this point, anyone else in the circle may quickly enter the scene and add something that would naturally be found next to or connected to a tree. For example, someone may run onstage, curl up into a ball at the foot of the "tree," and say, "I am an apple!" A third person then enters the scene, perhaps posing as a deer eating the apple under the tree and saying, "I am a deer!" Once a total of three people have entered the scene, the first performer quickly grabs one of the others by the hand and walks back into the circle. This leaves the third performer in the middle to strike up a new, perhaps unrelated pose and declare who or what they are, as before, with one and then another performer joining the scene again.

Hint

- Avoid explanations of relationships, such as "I am the deer eating the apple under the tree." Students should declare who or what they are and then freeze, leaving the interpretation of the relationship to the audience.

Side Coaching

- "Say who or what you are loudly and proudly!"
- "Don't think! What belongs next to that lawn mower? Create it."

Extension

- Add more people to the scenes. See if you can have the whole class create a set of interconnected organisms.

Grab Bag

Improv Level: Intermediate

Grade Level: 2nd grade and up

Time Needed: 20 minutes

Materials: Two bags filled with a variety of unusual objects connected with the science curriculum

This is a great activity to use at the beginning of a unit to allow students to play with new tools or objects. They will discover characteristics of each object that might otherwise be obscured when learning about the object's "true" purpose or function.

Directions

Two pairs of students (four students altogether) stand in front of the class. Each pair is given a bag with a collection of different objects. Students do not know what is in the bag until the activity begins. Each pair takes turns removing an object from the bag and quickly uses the object in some way. For example, one student might pull out a weather vane and place it on his partner's head, saying, "Don't forget your hat, sweetheart. It's going to be a cold one." The two pairs alternate for several turns and then another set of pairs is chosen to come onstage.

Hint

- The greater the variety of objects with regard to size and shape, the more successful this activity will be.

Side Coaching

- "Don't think about what the object really is. Make something up."
- "What's the first thing that comes into your head? Do that."

Extension

- Another version of this game can be done with the class seated in a circle. The bag is passed around the circle and one person at a time removes an object and says, "Your ____ is so ____," making up both a silly name and made-up descriptive word for the object. For example, if a magnifying glass is removed, the student might say, "Your flong is so smeathly!"

Metamorphosis

Improv Level: Beginner

Grade Level: All

Time Needed: 20 minutes

Materials: None

Life cycle changes are an important and often challenging concept for young science learners. The changes that organisms and environments experience throughout their lives cannot easily be seen and examined. With this exercise, students use their bodies to capture together the life cycle of an organism they are studying.

Directions

The class stands in a large circle. The class uses "Yes, and" to tell the story of the life cycle of an organism, such as a butterfly or a tree. For example, "An acorn fell from the big oak tree." Students are chosen to physically represent the different phases. The student who is assigned the initial life stage (a seed, a young caterpillar) arranges his or her body to represent the organism at that stage and then freezes in that position for the remainder of the exercise. The student to his or her left then represents the next stage and so on (ending with a mature tree or butterfly). The class can then look at the various poses they have created and discuss the changes they see represented in the circle.

Hint

- Students may have to hold a pose for several minutes. Choose students who will be able to be still for that long and encourage them to choose poses they will be comfortable holding for some time.

Side Coaching

- "Hold still!"

Extensions

- Start the story in different places to represent the fact that the life cycle does not have a beginning or an end.
- Have students re-create various events of their own day, with poses to represent getting dressed, walking to school, eating lunch, and so forth.

French Telephone

This fascinating activity demonstrates how change is always happening and how even the slightest changes within parts of a system affect the system as a whole. Students will be amazed at how the whole group changes what it is doing even though no one person is leading.

Improv Level: Beginner

Grade Level: 2nd grade and up

Time Needed: 15 minutes

Materials: None

Directions

Everyone stands in a circle. Each person chooses someone in the room whom they are to watch closely. This is done in a particular sequence. One student begins, choosing a student to watch by pointing to that student and saying his or her name. The chosen student then places a hand on her head to indicate that he or she has been chosen (and cannot be chosen again, keeping it there until everyone is chosen). She then chooses a student to watch in the same manner. This continues with everyone who is pointed to putting a hand on his or her head and pointing to another student, until everyone is chosen. Everyone in the room removes their hand from their head and stands as still and as silently as possible, carefully watching his or her chosen person. If someone moves in the slightest way (even the twitching of a finger), the person watching him or her must imitate that movement exactly. Eventually any subtle movement is transmitted around the room.

Hint

- Some students may be inclined to make intentional movements to make the game move more quickly. Explain to them that the game will be much more interesting if they genuinely try to keep still.

Side Coaching

- "Watch carefully. Be on the lookout for tiny offers."
- "Don't try to change, just imitate your partner."

Rain or Shine

Improv Level: Intermediate

Grade Level: All

Time Needed: 20 minutes

Materials: None

While we may follow a similar routine every day, how we go through our day changes depending on the weather. In this game students have a chance to replay everyday occurrences as though they were doing them in inclement weather or during a natural disaster. Repeating the scene in this way, students will be able to broaden their understanding of the impact these events have on people's lives.

Directions

A group of students begins by performing a short scene based on a typical event in their lives, such as playing kickball at recess or buying a hot dog from a street vendor. The scene is then replayed as before but now it is raining, or there is a hailstorm, an earthquake, a tornado, or a hurricane. When the students replay the scene, they have to change the action to accommodate the new environmental factor.

Hint

- Remind students to figure out who their characters are, what their relationship is, and what they are doing before changing the weather.

Side Coaching

- "What does it feel like?"
- "What's the temperature?"
- "How do you keep yourself from falling over?"

Extension

- This activity can be used with any kind of change—time of day, time of year, historical era, weightlessness, or age of characters.

Slide Show

Improv Level: Intermediate

Grade Level: 3rd grade and up

Time Needed: 30 minutes

Materials: None

One of the iconic characters of our culture is the brilliant scientist standing behind his projector giving an interminable lecture on mollusks (or some such subject). This activity plays with that idea by putting the students in the role of expert, and by bringing the slides to life. This not only helps students to develop their understanding of the performances of various professionals, it gives them an opportunity to creatively and collectively discover what they know about a subject and share it with their classmates.

Directions

One student is chosen to perform as the Expert who is presenting his slides from a recent research trip to a convention of interested scientists. Behind him onstage stand three to five other students who will perform as the Slides. The Expert begins his talk by introducing himself (e.g., Dr. Dino-mite) and his field of expertise (paleontology), and describes what the audience will see in the first Slide. Then he "clicks" an imaginary remote control for the "slide projector." When he does this, the students who are performing as the Slide must arrange themselves together into a shape or scene that represents what the expert was talking about. The group presents three or four Slides, and then another group of students has a turn.

Side Coaching

- To the students performing as the Slides: "There's no time to talk about what part you'll have. Look quickly for offers and then accept them. Freeze!"
- To the Expert: "Just start talking. You will discover that you have something to say."

Extension

- For a more challenging variation, have the students who are performing as the Slides first arrange themselves into an abstract shape while the Expert has his or her back to them. When the Expert clicks the remote, he or she must turn and then describe the Slide, justifying it as though it were a part of his or her presentation.

Chapter 7

More Advanced Scene Work

By this point we hope that many of you (and your students) have been bitten by the improv bug. If you have, this final chapter is for you. While we obviously think that improv has a value for academic learning, we also think it's just plain fun. This chapter is all about the joy of improvising. The activities we have provided will help students further develop as improvisers onstage and in life, able to create interesting and entertaining scenes that can, if you want, be put together into a show.

What do we mean by scene work? There are many different types of improv activities. There are games like "Woosh!" and "Sound Ball" that are essentially exercises for building and warming up the ensemble. There are activities like "Yes, and" that are used to develop particular improv skills. And there are activities where two or more people create a scene. There are many scene work activities scattered throughout the previous chapters. For example, both the "Three-Headed Expert" in Chapter 6 and "Captain Precision" in Chapter 5 are activities in which the performers create a scene. This final chapter contains more activities like those, most of which are quite challenging and require students to hone the skills they have been learning all along.

A note of caution for teachers of younger children: The activities in this chapter are probably more appropriate for upper elementary and middle school students. They require a high level of focus, some understanding of narrative structure, precision in the offers being made and picked up on, and an ability to make quick choices. However, as early childhood teachers know, young children often do these things in their free play, so if you're an early childhood teacher who wants to give the activities in this chapter a try, by all means do so.

Learning to create interesting improv scenes is inseparable from continuing to develop as an ensemble. In order for a scene to succeed, the ensemble has to give and receive offers, listen, say "yes, and," and work together to make sure *everyone* performs well. Creating scenes together can be an exhilarating experience—to collectively create a never-before-seen event, in just a few minutes, without any preplanning. For your students, it can sometimes feel like magic, but with the added benefit of knowing that they're the ones who created it!

While the activities in this chapter are not designed to teach to a specific curriculum area, children will continue to learn important academic skills. In particular, scene work helps children to develop their understanding of narrative structure. The most interesting scenes contain all the key elements of a good story: characters; location; interesting events; colorful moments; and a beginning, middle, and end. In the course of creating scenes, children will get better at seeing and supplying what is needed to keep the story moving and to help it come to a satisfying conclusion.

Many of the activities in this chapter can be used to teach or practice knowledge and skills from other areas of the curriculum. One way to do this is by limiting the content of the scene to a particular topic. For example, all the scenes in a "Freeze" sequence can be about the Revolutionary War, or the class can continue a basal reader story in "What Could Possibly Go Wrong?" We encourage teachers to be creative and continue to integrate improv into the curriculum, and we also hope that the activities in this chapter will be used to develop the ensemble's skill at theatrical performance.

As children have more experience creating scenes, they develop characters that can become a recurring part of the class's repertoire. They might create an old man, a baby, a surly teenager, and a brave superhero, and then use these characters in multiple scenes. While every scene will be different, children can bring these characters back again and again. Having the experience of creating characters that are both you and not you is invaluable—it helps children expand their repertoire of performances in their everyday lives. It teaches them that they do not have to be tied to one identity, and that they can create infinite performances of themselves.

PUTTING ON A SHOW!

One of the most exciting parts of improvising is putting on a show. While it can be a little scary and intimidating for students to get up onstage, there is a huge rush from performing for an audience. It is often in the activity of performing onstage that the ensemble is able to pull together everything they have been learning and, in Vygotskian terms, "perform ahead of where they are." Following are some suggestions for organizing an improv show.

A key piece of putting on a show is choosing the activities that the class will perform. For a show to be enjoyable for the audience and a positive experience for the class, attention should be paid to choosing activities that will be fun for your students and entertaining for an audience. Many of the activities in this book can work in a show, and all the ones in this chapter are appropriate for performance pieces. However, some of the games earlier in the book that are designed to teach or practice a particular skill (e.g., "Math-a-thon" or "Construct-o-Sentence"), or are exercises for developing the ensemble (e.g., "Woosh!" or "Sound Ball") are probably less interesting for an audience to watch. Choose activities where the performers have the potential to create an interesting scene

("What If?") or have a gimmick that makes it funny ("Emotional Bus"). That said, be creative. We can easily imagine a situation where parents would love to watch their 5-year-olds play "Sound Ball" or a group of 7th graders quickly create a storm in "Rain Noises." Over the course of learning to improvise, every ensemble develops some favorite activities. These are often excellent ones to put in a show because the children will enjoy sharing them with an audience. Finally, pick a few activities that are a stretch for your students because these will require them to use skills they are just learning. While they may not end up being the most successful scenes in the whole show, most audiences are appreciative of the hard work of learning to improvise and will enjoy seeing your students work to go beyond themselves.

Improv audiences have an important part to play during the show. They provide many of the suggestions that make the scenes unique. Your job as the director is to tell the audience what is expected of them. Let them know that you will be coming to them for anything from a location, to a title, to a relationship that two people might have (e.g., brother and sister). In addition, it is important to let the audience know that their job is to make the ensemble look good. One of our favorite improv directors famously started each show by declaring to the audience: "The more you laugh, the funnier we are." While it may sound ridiculous, it is actually true; an improv audience that is appreciating the show and giving that appreciation to the performers, actually transforms what the performers are able to do. Don't be afraid to teach the audience something about doing an "audience performance," as we discussed in Chapter 2.

In the excitement of performing for an audience, there is a tendency to forget that the unit that is performing is the ensemble. Children (and teachers) can become overly focused on being funny or being a star and forget that good improvisers do not go for the laugh at someone else's expense. The humor in improv is collectively created by the giving and receiving of offers. Before and during a show children might need to be reminded to figuratively say, "Yes, and" to their fellow performers. Finally, we have one last piece of advice about doing improv on and off the stage: Have fun!

What Could Possibly Go Wrong?

Improv Level: Intermediate

Grade Level: 3rd grade and up

Time Needed: 25 minutes

Materials: None

Everyone has had "one of those days" where one awful thing happens right after another, and we ask ourselves, "What else could possibly go wrong?" Other times, the phrase, "What could possibly go wrong?" famously precedes an unexpected, horrendous disaster. This activity allows students to creatively invent answers to those questions. The best part is, since the messes that get created will be imaginary, there'll be less cleaning up to do.

Directions

Three or more students are chosen to begin a scene. After a few minutes, the teacher interrupts them and asks the audience, "What could possibly go wrong?" Audience members offer suggestions of a mishap that could happen next in the scene. The performers then incorporate the new event and continue the scene.

Hint

- Scenes involving events unfolding in a sequence, such as a journey or the execution of a project, provide ample opportunities for the kinds of disasters that make this game work.

Side Coaching

- To the audience: "Make suggestions that include what you've *just* seen."

What If? (Scene Work Version)

Improv Level: Intermediate

Grade Level: 2nd grade and up

Time Needed: 20 minutes

Materials: None

Children (and many adults) spend countless hours wondering, "What if . . . ?" Sometimes these are elaborate fantasies and, other times, amusing little scenarios. In this exercise, students can find out the answers to their musings.

Directions

Three or more students are chosen to perform a short scene. Once completed, the performers ask the audience for a "What if?" suggestion. Suggestions might include:

- What if the scene took place under water?
- What if the whole family were cats?
- What if, when the waiter comes, José finds out he doesn't have any money?

The cast then plays the scene again, incorporating the suggestions. After a few minutes they stop again and ask for another suggestion. This continues as many times as the performers wish until the scene ends.

Hint

- Encourage students to make suggestions that change *how* the scene unfolds, rather than what events actually take place. The question "What if?" is not designed to prompt a new scene, but to add an element to the original scene.

Side Coaching

- "Stick with what happened the first time. Only change what would be different based on the audience's suggestion."

Freeze

Improv Level: Advanced

Grade Level: 2nd grade and up

Time Needed: 25 minutes

Materials: None

While we, as teachers, may often wish we could simply yell, "Freeze!" and have our students (and the rest of the world) respond, this trick only works in the world of fantasy. This game brings "Freeze" into the classroom. Students will enjoy how unrelated scenes seem to flow one from another.

Directions

Two students begin a scene. After a few minutes, another student can call, "Freeze!" and replace one of the performers by tapping her on the shoulder. The new performer then situates himself in the exact same position as the performer he is replacing. Once he is in place, the old performer calls out, "Action!" and a new scene begins.

Hints

- Keep the action moving by making transitions brief.
- New scenes are more easily created if they begin as though the characters were in the middle of a conversation or some piece of action.

Side Coaching

- "Keep moving. Pretend you're in the middle of a conversation."

Extension

- Surprise your students by calling out, "Freeze!" at other times of day, such as in the middle of a science lesson or when they are packing up to go home. Quickly cast a student to replace one of the frozen students and then "unfreeze" the scene and see what happens.

Options

Improv Level: Intermediate

Grade Level: 3rd grade and up

Time Needed: 25 minutes

Materials: None

Life is filled with choices. At any given moment we could stand on our heads, run around the room, or spend all of our money on a plane ticket to Borneo. We just never can tell what's around the corner. This exercise plays with the notion that anything can happen.

Directions

One student is chosen as a Director, three or more students are chosen to perform a scene, and the rest of the class is the Audience. The performers begin a scene. At any time during the scene, the Director freezes the action and asks a question, such as "What do they find in the bag?" or "Who's at the door?" The Audience offers suggestions and the scene continues.

Hint

- Look for suspenseful moments to ask for suggestions. This will further the action and keep the performers on their toes.

Secret

Improv Level: Advanced
Grade Level: 3rd grade and up
Time Needed: 25 minutes
Materials: Paper, markers, tape

This wacky, challenging scene plays on those moments where everyone seems to know something we don't.

Directions

Three students are chosen to perform a scene. They leave the room and the teacher solicits a suggestion for three different words, which will be written on paper and taped to each of the performers' backs, so that each one has a word on his or her back that the other players in the scene, and the audience, can see but that she or he cannot. The job of the performers is to create an improvised scene. As they do this, each of them attempts to get one another to say their word, which is hidden from them on their backs.

Hint

- While students may find this challenging, remind them that their attempts at getting their scene partners to say a particular word should be incorporated into the action and logic of the scene.

Side Coaching

- "Keep the scene moving. How can you creatively respond to the offers on the table *and* get your scene partner to say her word?"

Sitting, Standing, Kneeling

Improv Level: Advanced

Grade Level: 3rd grade and up

Time Needed: 25 minutes

Materials: None

This activity is an old improv standby. It's a challenging one because the performers must be hyperaware of their and their scene partners' positions at all times, and work to justify any changes into the logic of the scene.

Directions

Three students are chosen to perform a scene. They are free to create whatever they want, but at every moment one of them must be sitting, another standing, and a third kneeling. If a student who is kneeling stands up, the other characters must adjust their positions so their positions remain consistent with this rule.

Hint

- Until students are familiar with this game, set up the scene with a location that would logically include a chair and in which individuals might logically sit, stand, and kneel. Strong examples could include a doctor's office, a living room, or a preschool classroom.

Side Coaching

- "Remember, every move you make has to make sense in the scene."

Slow-Motion Olympics

Improv Level: Advanced

Grade Level: 2nd grade and up

Time Needed: 25 minutes

Materials: None

In the world of sports broadcasting, the slow-motion instant replay is reserved for only the finest of athletic maneuvers: the impossible catch, the gorgeous triple axel. This irreverent activity brings the world of instant replay and color commentaries to the most mundane activities.

Directions

Two students are chosen to perform a scene. They ask the audience for a suggestion of an everyday activity they can perform together. They then perform the scene in slow motion while a third performer provides commentary, as during a sports broadcast.

Hints

- Activities involving movement of the whole body, such as sweeping the floor, are more dramatic than those that involve only talking or slight movement, such as writing.
- For younger students, it may be necessary for the teacher to perform the difficult role of the commentator.

Side Coaching

- "Slower!"

Invisible Kickball

Improv Level: Advanced

Grade Level: 3rd grade and up

Time Needed: 25 minutes

Materials: Bases

This exercise is an excellent test of your class's ability to channel their competitive impulses toward competing on behalf of the group. If well executed, onlookers will wonder if your class has gone completely mad.

Directions

The entire class goes outside or to the gym, and is organized into teams for a game of kickball. They then begin playing the game, but with one twist—there's no ball. Students improvise a game, from start to finish, as they ordinarily would, using their imaginations to collectively create what happens.

Hints

- A desire on behalf of one or the other team to subvert the imaginary aspect of the game in order to "win" will prove disastrous. Remind students that although they're pretending to play a competitive game, they're actually engaged in an elaborate improv activity and that, as with all improv games, success depends on their competing on behalf of the group. Encourage students to fail (miss a catch, strike out) with great exuberance to add to the drama of the game.
- Another familiar activity that ordinarily involves a ball can be substituted for kickball.

Side Coaching

- "Stay with the scene. Remember, someone has to 'strike out.'"

Index of Improv Activities Listed by Level of Difficulty

Advanced

Index of Improv Activities Listed by Appropriate Age

Index of Improv Activities Listed by Other Relevant Subject Areas

Within the chapters, the improv activities are organized by the most relevant subject or activity heading. The following is a list of other subjects these activities may be relevant to.

Resources

IMPROVISATION AND DRAMA

Boal, A. (1993). *Games for actors and non-actors.* New York: Routledge.

Boal, A. (1995). *The rainbow of desire.* New York: Routledge.

Johnstone, K. (1981). *Impro: Improvisation and the theatre.* New York: Routledge.

Nachmanovich, S. (1990). *Free play: Improvisation in life and art.* New York: Putnam.

Polsky, M. (1998). *Let's improvise.* New York: Applause Theatre Books.

Sawyer, K. (1997). *Pretend play as improvisation: Conversations in the preschool classroom.* Mahwah, NJ: Lawrence Erlbaum.

Spolin, V. (1999). *Improvisation for the theater* (3rd ed.). Chicago: Northwestern University Press.

Timpson, W., & Burgoyne, S. (2002). *Teaching and performance: Ideas for energizing your classes.* Madison, WI: Atwood Publishing.

VYGOTSKY

Daniels, H. (1996) *An introduction to Vygotsky.* Mahwah, NJ: Routledge.

Dixon-Krauss, L. (1995) *Vygotsky in the classroom: Mediated literacy instruction and assessment.* New York: Allyn & Bacon.

Goncu, A. (1999). *Children's engagement in the world: Sociocultural perspectives.* Cambridge, UK: Cambridge University Press.

Holzman, L. (1997). *Schools for growth.* London: Routledge.

Kozulin, A., & Gindis, B. (2003). *Vygotsky's educational theory in cultural context.* Cambridge, UK: Cambridge University Press.

Mooney, C. (2000). *Theories of childhood: An introduction to Dewey, Montessori, Erikson, Piaget & Vygotsky.* New York: Redleaf Press.

Newman, F., & Holzman, L. (1993). *Lev Vygotsky: Revolutionary scientist.* New York: Routledge

Vygotsky, L. (1978). *Mind in society: The development of higher psychological processes.* Boston: Harvard University Press.

Vygotsky, L. (1962). *Thought and language.* Cambridge, MA: MIT Press.

Wells, G. (1999). *Dialogic inquiry: Towards a socio-cultural practice and theory of education.* Cambridge, UK: Cambridge University Press.

Wink, J., & Putney, L. (2001). *A vision of Vygotsky.* Upper Saddle River, NJ: Prentice Hall.

GROUPS AND GROUP LEARNING

Kagan, S. (1993). *Cooperative learning.* San Clemente, CA: Kagan Cooperative Learning

John-Steiner, V. (2000). *Creative collaboration.* New York: Oxford.

Rogoff, B. (1998). Cognition as a collaborative process. In D. Kuhn & R. S. Siegler (Eds.), *Handbook of child psychology, 5th ed., Vol. 2: Cognition, perception, and language* (pp. 679–744). New York: Wiley.

IMAGINATION, CREATIVITY, AND THE ARTS

Armstrong, T. (1998). *Awakening genius in the classroom.* Washington, DC: Association for Supervision and Curriculum Development.

Cropley, A. (2002). *Creativity in education and learning: A guide for teachers and educators.* London: Kogan Page Limited.

Egan, K. (1989). *Teaching as storytelling: An alternative approach to teaching and curriculum in the elementary school.* Chicago: University of Chicago Press.

Egan, K. (2005) *An imaginative approach to teaching.* San Francisco: Jossey-Bass.

Eisner, E. (1998). *The kinds of schools we need: Personal essays.* Portsmouth, NH: Heinemann.

Eisner, E. (2004). *The arts and the creation of mind.* New Haven, CT: Yale University Press.

Fowler, C. (2002). *Strong arts, strong schools: The promising potential and shortsighted disregard of the arts in American schooling.* Oxford, UK: Oxford University Press.

Greene, M. (2000). *Releasing the imagination: Essays on education, the arts, and social change.* San Francisco: Jossey-Bass.

Greene, M. (2001). *Variations on a blue guitar: The Lincoln Center Institute series on aesthetic education.* New York: Teachers College Press.

Hoffman-Davis, J. (2005). *Framing education as art: The octopus has a good day.* New York: Teachers College Press.

Lynch, M., & Harris, C. R. (2000). *Fostering creativity in children, K–8: Theory and practice.* New York: Allyn and Bacon.

Meador, K. (1997). *Creative thinking and problem solving for young learners.* Englewood, CO: Teacher Idea Press.

Powell, M., & Speiser, V. (2005). *The arts, education, and social change: Little signs for change.* New York: Peter Lang.

Thousand, J., Villa, R., & Nevin, A. (2002). *Creativity and collaborative learning: The practical guide to empowering students, teachers, and families* (2nd ed.). Baltimore, MD: Paul H. Brookes.

INTERNET RESOURCES

www.performingtheworld.org
www.performanceofalifetime.com
www.humanpingpongball.com/
www.learnimprov.com/
www.unexpectedproductions.org/playbook.htm
www.yesand.com
www.claquetheatre.com/theatre_games.htm

About the Authors

Carrie Lobman, Ed.D., is Assistant Professor of Education at the Graduate School of Education, Rutgers University. Carrie has been an educator in the New York metropolitan area for over 20 years. She was a founding member of the improv ensemble Laughing Matters, and has written several articles on the relationship between improv and teaching. In 2006, she helped launch an improv training program for teachers called the Developing Teachers Fellowship Program at the East Side Institute for Group and Short Term Therapy. She received her MSEd. from Hunter College at the City University of New York and her Ed.D. from Teachers College, Columbia University.

Matthew Lundquist, MSSW, MSEd., is a social therapist, the Director of the Manhattan Social Therapy Group, and an educational consultant. A former New York City special education teacher, learning specialist, and school social worker, Matthew brings improvisation and performance to his work with children, adults, families, and teachers. Matthew is an adjunct instructor at the Hunter College School of Social Work. He received his MSSW from the Columbia University School of Social Work and his MSEd. from Bank Street College of Education.